CW00701450

Memoir

Cameras: my life
through and behind the lens

By George Schoenmann

Published 2012 by Mulfran Press
2 Aber Street, Cardiff CF11 7AG
UK
www.mulfran.co.uk

ISBN 1-907327-17-9

Printed by imprint**digital** in Devon [info@imprintdigital.net].

Contents

Introduction

After completing volumes 1 and 2 of my memoirs, I still felt that there was one important aspect of my life that had not been covered and that is the part photography and cameras have played. So I am hoping that once this work is committed to print the trilogy is complete, my literary aspirations achieved and a record of my life's work duly recorded for posterity.

I am sure the interest in photography is hereditary as my father was an enthusiastic photographer. I shall therefore start the story at the time when I came on the scene in 1934 and deal as best I can with his photographic history from that date. Luckily he was very methodical and put most of his photographs into albums with comments and dates, so has made the task relatively easy for me. During the painful war years (for him that is rather than for me) photography almost came to a stop for two reasons: lack of film and lack of a camera since his was confiscated for the duration of hostilities.

After his premature enforced retirement and health problems, he devoted his time and energies to stamp collecting, building up a magnificent collection of stamps, pre-stamp letters and postcards. Unfortunately this interest did not come down through the genes and I never had any interest in stamps except very briefly as a schoolboy. So after his death in 1967, I had custody of the collection and for more than thirty years it stayed untouched in my study. About ten years ago my sister Helly and brother-in-law Alan said that we ought to do something with it, and they undertook the task of selling the collection. It had to be done carefully in sections, through philatelic auctions rather than just handing the whole lot to a dealer, and in this way they achieved a very creditable result and fair price.

At about this time my interest in old cameras was awakened, starting with Helly giving me my father's last camera, the Retina Reflex. As I very seldom sold any of my old cameras, I had the basis of a collection. During my retirement collecting cameras has become my main hobby or obsession as the family call it. I categorically deny being addicted to e-bay but as may be expected, this subject will be dealt with in depth towards the end of the memoirs.

Anyway, I feel that the cost has been covered by the proceeds of the stamp collection, so do not feel too guilty about the money spent. Hopefully the cameras will prove as good an investment as the stamp collection was for my father. Old cameras are a very collectible item and will not lose their value, because when they disappear into private collections they are effectively being taken off the market. As a result their numbers get fewer and fewer each year. Well, that is my theory anyway………….

I hope my readers will enjoy my reminiscences as much as I have enjoyed writing them.

Dedications

To my father, for passing on his enthusiasm and knowledge.
And in a roundabout way providing the funds to enable me to
pursue my collecting ambitions without feeling too guilty about
the cost.

To Jill, Julietta and Angelina for being the subject matter, and
to Clara and Freya for all they may have to endure in the
future, now that the enthusiasm has passed to their own father.
Thank you all.

Summer 2012

Chapter 1: pre-war in Vienna

I have been trying to unravel the history of the cameras my father had at the time that I arrived on the scene in August 1934, but have not been able to come to any positive conclusion. Most of my knowledge is based on what he told me on our Sunday morning walks - just the two of us - when we were told to 'clear off' while my mother got the lunch ready. As I recall we usually headed off down to the old canal which ran alongside the Melingriffith Iron and Tinplate works, and then along the railway line which linked it to the main railway at Taffs Well. If we were lucky we even met a train, but they were pretty rare on a Sunday. It was on these walks that he told me about his earlier life in Vienna, his period of service in the Austrian army and his time as a prisoner of war in Italy. All this goes back nearly 70 years, but as much as he told me has stuck pretty firmly: the hard bit is making it all fit with the evidence I have to hand.

am ersten Morgen

The German script says "On the first morning".

I was already at that age interested in cameras, and two models were most often mentioned - the Zeiss Cocarette, and the Icarette. Unfortunately I just cannot be sure which he had at the time of my birth. My usual sources of information are the photo albums and making judgements based on the size of the pictures. The earliest pictures taken in the nursing home soon after birth were definitely taken with a roll-film camera, as they are all contact prints and consistent with the negative size for one of these cameras. Later in the album is a picture of me holding a camera case, which again bears this out.

Looking further through the pictures, I find that the print size changes after about 4 months. I am certain this indicated that my father had bought a new camera and I am sure this was a Retina 1 which he often spoke about. I know this camera came on the market in 1934 and probably after some time became available in the shops. The next picture is one of the earliest Retina pictures in the book.

The Retina Type 117

This picture is entitled "Father and son".

As flash was still many years away, nearly all of his pictures are taken with 'available light', which shows that whoever took the picture had a very steady hand, bearing in mind that the lens was f.3.5, and the film speed 25 or 50 ASA (for the technical amongst you). I am fortunate enough to have an original Retina in the collection although it is not his actual camera.

Another now infamous picture that he took is reproduced below. This has been the cause of much hilarity among the family and may explain the Schoenmann obsession with toilets.

A picture I am still ashamed of.

In 1935 my father went on a business trip to visit his customers in Portugal and for reasons which were never fully explained, decided to take his sister Hannah rather than my mother. I assume my mother had her hands full with me and, although we had a nurse maid and a housemaid, she probably felt that she did not want to leave me either with them or with grandparents. As they were visiting their customers in Lisbon (which was one of their company's main export markets) and Aunt Hannah had worked in the family business before her marriage, the whole trip could hopefully be classed as a business trip, and so written off against profits. I am pleased to say Jill and I did most of our travelling on the same basis. There is a lot to be said for owning your own company. But we never had any qualms about leaving the children with grandparents......

There is a complete album devoted to this trip and their route took them by train to Paris, then to Oporto and Lisbon. There are pictures taken in Seville and other seaside towns on Spain's Atlantic coast until they reached Gibraltar. There they boarded the SS Roma, which was the pride of Italy at the time. From there they sailed to Naples, saw Pompeii, and on to Sorrento. A journey which we did on holiday in 2009. From there they went to Palermo on the north coast of Sicily and then round the island to Ragusa on the south coast, a journey we also covered in 2008. There are some pictures showing the harbour of Patras which is in Greece and a long way off the route. They finally ended the trip in Trieste which was presumably the nearest port to Austria. I think the whole journey took four or even six weeks and they certainly covered a lot of Europe. Unfortunately my father was much keener on taking landscape pictures than people and family (apart from pictures of me). Sixty or seventy years later, future generations are much keener on seeing pictures of people and it is such a pity that there are so few pictures in the albums of my ancestors.

The SS Roma, Pride of Italy

My father and Aunt Hannah playing cards on the Roma.
It is a pity the chap taking the air has lost his head!

In 1937 my father started a new picture album and I think this must have coincided with the purchase of a new camera. I know that when we came to Great Britain in 1939 he had a Zeiss Ikon Super Nettel, and as this came on the market in 1936 I think he must have bought it as soon as it was out. The fate of the Retina will be dealt with later.

The Zeiss Ikon Super Nettel

The Super Nettel was introduced by Zeiss to appeal to amateur photographers who wanted a quality 35mm camera, but could not quite afford the top of the range Contax models that were on offer. It was also a folding camera and so could fit in a (large) pocket. It had the same focal plane shutter as the Contax and a four element Tessar f.2.8 lens. It also had a rotating wedge coupled rangefinder. I bought one of these very early in my collecting phase as I wanted to own and handle one. I was lucky to find a very clean example at Photographica in 2002.

In 1937 my parents went for a summer holiday again on a ship. They took my Aunt Hannah with them but left me behind, although to be fair I don't think I would have appreciated a cruising holiday at that age. The ship was Italian - the MV Puccini. Looking through the album to retrace their journey I see that they had an overnight stop in Venice, the clue being night pictures of St Mark's Square. The next stopover was Milan and then on to Genoa where they picked up the ship. It was a small tramp ship of about 3000 tons. It called at the main ports on Italy's western seaboard: Livorno, Pisa, Naples and then finally Malta. There are many pictures taken in the Grand Harbour, all of them very familiar to us as we spent a week there last year and stood in exactly the same spots. In 75 years very little seems to have changed, despite all the bombing which destroyed so much of the town. It seems to have been rebuilt very much as it was then. Up to this point the pictures are captioned, but after this there are none and I cannot recognise the places they went to. I would guess that they went up the eastern side and ended in Trieste again, mainly because the harbour pictures look the same as in 1935 when the Roma journey finished there.

My mother and Aunt Hannah (on the left) relaxing at sea

The MV Puccini in the Grand Harbour Valetta, Malta

The standard of photographs taken with the new camera seem to have improved too, and the album devoted to me traces my childhood up until July 1937 with his witty captions. After this the captions are missing although there are still many more pictures, including some taken on a summer holiday which looks to me as though we went to Velden. This was a place frequently referred to in my second volume of memoirs where we went often in the early post war period. Moreover I went with Jill in 1964 and later our children in 1970 and 1979. I am making this supposition based on the fact that when we went to Velden after the war (for the first time in 1949) and having passed through Klagenfurt, the capital of Carinthia, we came to a small place at the eastern end of the Worthersee called Krumpendorf. My father asked my mother if she remembered the last occasion that they had passed through and wondered if she recalled a huge sign announcing *Keine Juden in Krumpendorf* (No Jews in Krumpendorf). And this was still in 1937, many months before the Nazis marched into Austria, but shows the mindset of the Austrians at that time. The next picture is the penultimate in the album and shows my grandfather - probably the last picture of him ever taken.

Happier times in Vienna, although I look pretty worried

The last picture of me holding the exposure meter, of which I was inordinately fond, judging by the frequency with which it appears in the pictures

After this there are no more pictures, not even any recording the birth of my sister Helly on December 27th 1937, an event I would have thought was worth photographing. But of course there was much else to occupy him at the time, and in 1938 the Nazis marched into Austria and announced that they were annexing it with Germany, and were cheered to the rafters by the local population. Life for the Jews in Austria would never be the same again and the happy days were truly over.

Life for my parents during the last year after the *Anschluss* on March 12th 1938, and until we were allowed to leave in April 1939, must have been incredibly difficult. I can only imagine that my parents kept off the streets as much as possible and outings to the park in Hietzing, with its miniature village and model railway were a thing of the past. I am sure photography was the last thing on my father's mind, and saving the lives of his family became the foremost.

Chapter 2: war time in Whitchurch

Moving on to our life in Whitchurch in the early years of the war is a period where I have some actual memories. I have practically no recollection of my pre-war life in Vienna and most of what I know is based on hearsay and looking at the old pictures. There are very few photographs of children or family life to my knowledge. A simple reason for this is that Austrians were classed as *enemy-aliens* and would-be spies. For this reason most of the males were interned on the Isle of Man for quite a long period. Another edict saw all cameras and radios being confiscated and a curfew imposed. My father escaped the internment as he was deemed to be essential to the running of his factory, and so excused. Other members of our family were not so fortunate, and quite how the dependants of internees were meant to support themselves when the main breadwinner was taken away is still a mystery to me. I can only assume the families all helped each other as I am sure there were no handouts from the state to refugees back in those days. But everyone was glad to have escaped with their lives from the Nazi tyranny and no-one complained.

I have an album of pictures which my father took of his factory which I think were for publicity purposes. Yet I am at a loss to explain how he took these pictures when he had no camera? I can only conjecture based on a few other memories that come back to me....I can recall that for a period there was a Retina very similar to the one first mentioned in the previous chapter - this was kept in the cupboard with his other photographic equipment. I am wondering if perhaps this was a camera belonging to my uncle Erich (who was his brother-in-law and married to Aunt Hannah) who had been sent to the Isle of Man. I think perhaps he did not hand it over when the police called and had given it to my father for safekeeping. I also wonder if possibly this was his original Retina and he may have given it to Erich when he bought the Super Nettel? Who knows? We can but speculate. Certainly the existence of the Retina was never discussed or spoken about which makes me think that it was 'illegal'.

The pictures of the factory are admirable and a credit to the Retina, if indeed that was the camera used. I know they are his enlargements and I assume that if a professional had been called in to take them, then the photographer would have produced the prints and probably not used a 35mm camera. I reproduce a selection herewith.

The gumming and slitting machine with heated roller and bobbins

The folding room where bobbins were cut and folded to the correct size

A packaging machine which packed 60 sheets into the familiar Rizla packets

The hand packing room where different size packets were made. The gentleman with the bow tie is the department manager

Box packing room, where 200 packets were put into boxes for final despatch

I have also recently discovered (well, more accurately my sister had custody of a box of old photographs and I have been able to copy a selection) more pictures which must have been taken during the war, and assume these were taken with the Retina. I was 11 when the war ended and but look younger in the pictures. There were also some pictures taken on our Sunday morning walks around the Melingriffith tinplate factory, and I thought these were worth printing as it is all very different now.

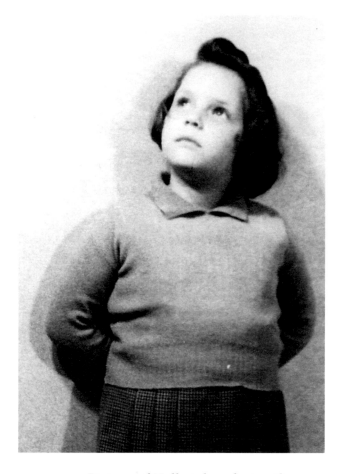

Picture of Helly taken during the war.

Another picture that I think was taken during war-time with the 'illegal' camera

Above is the old Glamorganshire canal

*The entrance to the Melingriffith Works and
bridge over the canal*

Photography for my father did not come to a complete halt though, as he still had his enlarger, which came over from Vienna in the two railway wagons that the Nazis mysteriously allowed out of the country. We had a darkroom set up in the small spare bedroom in the house on The Parade in Whitchurch and I was his willing helper. I was allowed to handle the prints in the developing dish - washing them and finally putting them in the fixer. All my basic knowledge came from my role as a 'helper'. Although film was in very short supply during the war years photographic paper, although very expensive, was obtainable. Likewise the chemicals. My father spent a lot of time enlarging the best pictures from his pre-war travels and I have the album he produced. Significantly it is titled *Seen through the lens.*

Chapter 3: the Gnome connection

My father was greatly helped in his photography by his friendship with Mr H. Loebstein, the owner of Gnome Photographic Products. Mr Loebstein was a refugee from Nazi Germany and before the war had a company in, I think, Nurenberg making mainly enlargers. He arrived in Cardiff at roughly the same time as we did, possibly a bit earlier, and set up a small company right in the centre of Cardiff at 21A Working Street. The site is now buried under the St David's shopping centre. There he made very big enlargers for the photographic trade and, during the war, for the War Department. As photographic reconnaissance was very important to the RAF his products were in huge demand, and the company did very well. Very soon after the war ended, Gnome moved to a new factory in Caerphilly Road, Birchgrove and started to produce new products for use by amateurs. Following are some of their adverts that I found on the internet:

This shows the variety of products Gnome was offering in 1946

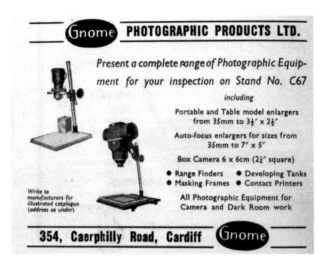

This advertisement is from 1949 and the enlarger on the left is the one I still have

I don't think my father ever had to pay for anything as Mr Loebstein gave the item to him to try out and never asked for it back. I am sure my father gave him all the cigarette paper he needed in exchange, and they certainly got through quite a lot of cognac - which was their favourite tipple - no matter what time of day but usually a Saturday or Sunday morning. The air was so thick with smoke that you needed fireman's breathing apparatus to go in. They never thought to open a window. Unfortunately the smoking had a price, and the grim reaper took them both well before they reached their allotted span of three score years and ten. Another item I have which I think was a prototype that never made it into production was a colour slide projector, made from solid aluminium castings and using a 12 volt car headlight bulb. I am sure it was never produced due to the lack of cooling: as the body got so hot it became a serious health hazard, especially if you happened to touch the body after a slide show lasting an hour or more. We also had quite a useful slide viewer and all my father's slides were in the

Gnome steel holders. They also made a range of cheap enlargers under the name of Alpha and Beta and every keen, but not too wealthy, photographer had one of those. I did too, but sold it in 1967 when I inherited all the darkroom equipment after my father's sad death.

The 35mm enlarger, shown here in its carrying case and assembled.

It had two extension tubes (one of which came with the enlarger) and the longer one my father had made so that he could produce 16"x 12" pictures. If you wanted even bigger enlargements you turned the enlarger through 180 degrees and projected on to the floor. The wired-in timer is also shown plus the transformer which is used to run the 12 volt car headlight bulbs. The same was needed for the projector below:

The projector that I am sure never went into production.

Gnome metal slide holders and the boxes which held 24. The boxes were of such good quality that they are still like new 60 years later. Overleaf is the quite useful slide viewer if one only wanted to look at pictures alone.

The Gnome Sprite projector which I still have, and seldom use any more.

This is the last Gnome item I acquired in 1977, although I had to actually pay some money for this. For a 2 year period during my time at Controller Contacts I had a young man called Paul as my assistant. He had spent several years working at Gnome as a draughtsman and he managed to buy it for me at 'trade price'. It was useful because it could take normal magazines which held 36 slides as well as circular drums that held 122. This was one of their cheaper models that worked by manual operation of the slider mechanism. To be honest, I was never a great colour slide enthusiast, as the task of setting up the screen and projector meant that by the time it had all been done, the already yawning audience were less than enthusiastic to watch the slides. As soon as colour prints became affordably cheap to process I changed over to them and the slide equipment has lain unused and unloved in the attic ever since. How easy it is today when a memory stick plugs straight into the back of the TV set, and you can show your photographs with the minimum of disruption to your eager - or maybe not-so-eager - audience.

Going back to the time before I left home in the mid-fifties, my father decided that he would make his own Christmas cards and I was his lab assistant in the production process. As he sent out about 200 every year this was quite a task. But with him on the enlarger and me doing the developing we soon got through them. He had devised a method of putting a black frame around the print and, especially with a snow scene, this looked quite classy. On other pictures though it looked somewhat funereal. He did this by first placing a piece of black card (which was just smaller than the intended picture) inside the masking frame and taking the negative carrier out, then exposing for a few seconds with white light only. We had an electric drier for the prints to stop them curling which happens when they dry naturally. They then had to be fixed to the pre-printed Christmas cards using a dry-mounting paper and my mother's iron. They looked quite professional when finished and greatly admired by all his friends and relatives. In the fifties Gnome made a camera called the Pixie, using 120 films and this was quite successful. I have found a picture of Helly holding her camera.

31

Helly with her Pixie camera taken on the Parade in Whitchurch.

They went on to make a Pixieflex which was a homage to the Rollieflex, but with a very simple specification. Unfortunately Kodak was making something very similar in plastic, at a much lower price, but neither sold particularly well, as the design was a pretty pointless exercise. The cameras did not need focusing, and for viewing you got an equally good result using the open frame finder. They also made a Baby Pixie, giving sixteen (rather than twelve) smaller pictures on the same 120 format film. The Pixie cameras were made from 1947 to 1952. The pictures below are from McKeown's Camera book.

Pixie Model I (1949) - 1949. Black crackle-finish enamel. Shutter release on lower right side of body. $15-25.

Baby Pixie Model III (1951) - c1951. Later
version has leatherette covering and black
finish. Shutter release on top right side of
body. $20-30.

Baby Pixie Model IV (1950)

Pixie-Flex - c1950. Pseudo-TLR for
6x6cm exposures on 620 film. Large
hooded ground glass finder. Better model

Gnome also ventured into offering 35mm cameras but were not
successful. They imported a camera from Germany made by

Adox and put a Gnome logo over the original Adox nameplate. They chose one of Adox's simpler cameras, but they were selling them against much better specified cameras from world famous German makers such as Zeiss Ikon and Kodak Retina, as well as Agfa and Voigtlander. The whole 35mmm camera venture did not last long and was discontinued. Once colour prints became affordable and home enlarging began to decline, Gnome concentrated on making slide projectors. In the latter years of their existence they took over Elite Optical, who made epidiascopes and overhead projectors which sold well to schools. The company finally closed as the eighties turned into the nineties. The factory was pulled down and is now the car park for a supermarket. *Sic transit*.................

Chapter 4: the early post-war years

The war finally ended in 1945 and I am sure my father's camera was returned by the authorities who had confiscated it. My father did not keep it very much longer and in 1946 changed it for a Contax 11. I clearly remember when he brought it home from London, where he had bought it in Wallace Heaton in New Bond Street, then the most famous camera shop in Britain. I even remember the price he paid - £108 (about £3000 in today's money) although he probably got a very good trade-in allowance on the Super Nettel. The camera must have been at least 6 years old as none were imported during the war years, and production had hardly restarted at the factories. These were located in Dresden and almost destroyed during the infamous raids just before the end of the war. Such was the shortage of cameras that really crazy prices were being asked, and obviously achieved. The cameras are still expensive today, despite being 60 years old. I paid £160 for the one shown below which is in my collection.

A Contax 11 from my collection.

Unfortunately there are very few pictures to be found that were taken with this camera, although it went on many holidays. As will be related in subsequent chapters, I had my own camera and all the pictures I have from these holidays I took myself. My father seemed to have lost his enthusiasm for putting pictures into albums during this period, as of course it was an increasingly fraught time for him during the late forties and very early fifties: he was ousted from his own company by the new owners to whom his fellow shareholders had sold their shares. I will deal with my adventures with this camera a little later too. Among the box of his remaining pictures, I found one of yours truly clutching our beloved cat. She gloried in the name of 'Pussy' and lived with us for nigh-on 20 years, produce a litter about twice a year for most of them. She was indeed a highly productive cat – clearly very popular with the local tomcat population - and lived on top of the gas fridge, the warmest spot in the kitchen.

"Pussy"

In 1958, my father decided to buy a new camera and changed his allegiance back to Kodak. The Retina Reflex had just been announced, and despite Zeiss having an almost comparable model available, settled for this. The Retina was definitely superior to the Zeiss offering, especially as regards the lens. The Retina was available with a six-element f.2.0/50 Xenon, whereas the Contaflex only offered a 4-element f.2.8/50 Tessar. Both had interchangeable front elements with wide angle and telephoto lenses available. But he was never enthusiastic about carrying a bag full of extra lenses. The camera is very fully specified, with a coupled selenium cell meter, and a split-image rangefinder. He had some sort of business deal going with Kodak and could buy equipment at 'trade price', whatever that may mean. In those days there was Retail Price Maintenance in force and getting discounts on anything was a rarity.

I am glad to say the actual camera has found its way back to my collection, and I am pleased and proud to have it. When my father died in 1967, it was very traumatic for me personally; I felt I did not want to take anything that was his and it should all stay with my mother. She asked me if I wanted it and (possibly this was only a day or two after he had died and much too soon) I said I would not take it as I had a camera - albeit a far inferior one. I think my sister also refused, and so my mother eventually gave it to the son of her friend and business partner in Vienna, Turhan Sellahattin. He was into photography in a big way, but preferred Nikons and more sophisticated cameras than the Retina. He did however have it repaired and serviced, because he said it was not working properly. When Helly and Alan went to Vienna to visit him many years later, he gave it back to them as he did not really want it. Alan had a Retinette which he was happy with, so it did not get used by him either. Eventually as my camera collection took shape in 2006 they gave it to me; it came to me 39 years after I was first offered it.

The Retina reflex. This is my father's actually camera

The camera was used for business too, taking the pictures of the kitchen furniture that my father's company Esto Products Ltd made. These pictures formed the main sales literature used by all the companies agents, and me their only employed representative.

Pictures from the Esto Catalogue.

These pictures were also the basis for the brochures when they became coloured line drawings. The camera was also used to take our wedding pictures, as our 'budget' wedding precluded hiring a professional photographer. Fortunately the cost of a wedding does not affect the quality of the marriage!

Our wedding, April 4th 1959, at Llandough Church.

I also have an album recording the trip my parents made to South America in 1960. Sad to say this was just when the situation at my father's factory was going rapidly downhill, but he was probably feeling fully recovered from the sciatica and teeth problems which had hit him a short time before. These had necessitated a period of total bed rest for three months or more and a full anaesthetic operation in the infirmary to remove all his teeth. I do feel that he tended to assume all was well, and was certainly not aware of the criminal activity that was going on in the business. Sadly it collapsed by the end of that year when Barclay's Bank refused to extend their overdraft. The main purpose of their visit was so that my mother could visit her family, most of whom were based in Sao Paulo. My grandmother had been 'exiled' there, after all the rows with my father, mainly centred on the fact that she would not look after her grandchildren alone in the house. He was not known for his propensity for forgiveness. In 1949 he decided that he had done his share of supporting her for the last 10 years, and packed her off to go and live with her son, my Uncle Fritz, in Sao Paulo. This almost broke my poor mother's heart, and I think the marriage must have rocked on its foundations.

Uncle Fritz supported her for the next 25 years as she lived to be nearly 90. Of course at the time of all this upheaval I was away at boarding school, so was totally oblivious. He took the Retina with him to Brazil and came back with a superb collection of pictures. He also decided to try his hand with a movie camera and through his contacts with Kodak, acquired a very basic Brownie cine camera. He took about 20 rolls of film but never bought a projector. His friend Mr Wilde was a great cine enthusiast, and had all the equipment, so he edited them and put them on a big reel. I have that too, but have only watched it twice, as it is quite hard going and not exactly riveting stuff. My main criticism is that cheap 8mm cameras do not lend themselves to landscape work. They are much better for pictures of people. My father was not a 'people person'- if only he had realised that what future generations would want to see is pictures of people. In the whole album there is only one picture of my mother, and absolutely none of anyone else in the family. A sad omission indeed.

The liner *Aragon* took them from Southampton to Cherbourg, then Vigo in Spain, and Lisbon in Portugal. Then across the Atlantic to Bahia, where they visited my Great Uncle Gustav Epstein, who did the famous sketch of my father. He was an artist of some renown, and made a good living by selling his paintings of the Indigenous Brazilians. From there it was on to Rio and then Sao Paulo. They flew to Brasilia, which was then in the early stages of construction, and looked more like a giant building site, rather than a capital city. They came home by air on a De Havilland Comet.

My father as drawn by Gustav Epstein

My mother and her luggage at Cardiff
General Station (now Central Station).

The Royal Mail Steamship 'Aragon' at Cherbourg

Rio de Janeiro

A beach in Rio

Sao Paulo

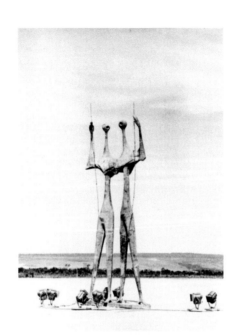

Brasilia, still in the course of being built

The BOAC Comet for the flight home.

My parents still made one major trip, taking the car on a passenger ship to Rome and then driving back. I cannot find any pictures, except colour slides taken mainly when they spent some time with my sister Helly in Grundelwald. They went on the Jungfrau railway to the summit and some excellent pictures were taken.

My mother and Helly in the Cafe at the Summit of the Jungfrau

Pictures of the Jungfraubahn Railway.

The Jungfrau itself.

Chapter 5: early camera ownership

Turning now to my own life with cameras, I can truthfully say that I cannot positively remember when my father gave me my first camera. I think it most likely was an 11th birthday present, which just about coincided with the end of the war. I do not even know where he bought the camera, but assume he got it from his friend Randall Cox who had the more prominent of the two camera shops in Cardiff at the time (the other being Salanson's in Queen Street). Randall Cox was in the Duke Street Arcade and I spent a fair amount of time studying the goodies he had on offer in his window.

The camera is a Zeiss Ikon Baby Box Tengor, dating from 1931-34, slightly older than I was at the time. This was a wise choice on his part, as the camera was much better specified than the average box camera and had a focusing 3-element f.6.3 Novar lens, and a simple shutter giving Instantaneous, Time and Brief exposures. The wire frame at the front of the viewfinder was pressed into the body when not in use, and this locked the shutter to avoid accidental exposures. The camera took 16 pictures size 3 X 4 cm on 127 film. From somewhere he had obtained a roll of film too - quite an achievement at the time. Having these simple settings meant that I had to judge both the exposure and set the focus which were useful lessons, rather than just point and shoot as most beginner's cameras required.

The Baby Box Tengor. Unfortunately this is not the actual camera, which I sold at some time.

Luckily, quite a few pictures I took with the camera have survived because I had the foresight to stick them in an album, and write the relevant date and place where they were taken. All the pictures are in contact print form as I also was given two printing frames. I was able to enlarge some of them, but not very successfully as the negatives were just not good enough. Photoshop was a little more successful, but it is just not possible to improve what is not there.

My father in 1948, and below, the newly built factory

Our house at 14, The Parade, Whitchurch

Picture taken in 1948 on our first ever holiday in Brittany.
The harbour is Port Haligon, on the Quiberon Peninsular

The Liner Liberte in dock at St Nazaire.

This ship really caught my imagination. It was a German liner, SS Europa, which was used by the Americans as a troop ship to return forces from Europe. It was then given to the French as a prize of war. It sunk in Le Havre, was raised, and towed to St Nazaire, which is where we saw it. In 1930 it held the Blue Riband for the fastest crossing of the Atlantic. It caught fire soon after this picture was taken, but was repaired, and served as the French flag-ship until the SS France was built in 1960 (see Wikipedia)

The Eiffel Tower, shortly before we went to the top

1949, our first visit to Vienna

Somewhere in the Alps, my father with his Contax 11

Mont Blanc, taken from Chamonix, during my enforced idleness due to my Athlete's foot.

A picture taken probably at the same time. I apologise for the poor quality, but they are very old

Chapter 6: the start of 35mm photography and time (mis)spent at university

In 1951 for my seventeenth birthday my parents gave me a 35mm camera, as they must have thought that my enthusiasm for photography deserved encouragement. The camera they bought was an Akarette 11. At that time new cameras were still in very short supply in Great Britain and were very expensive due to import duties and purchase tax. So rather unwisely they bought the camera in Austria, probably during our holiday in Velden the previous summer. They managed to keep it secret and I was really delighted. Unfortunately when we re-entered the UK they somehow 'forgot' to tell HM Customs about it, and so although it could be used in Britain, it could not be taken abroad again as there was no tax receipt available.

The Akarette 11

The camera was made by a newly established company called Apparat und Kamerabau GmbH of Friedrichshafen in West Germany. It was almost unique in having a fully interchangeable lens and a leaf shutter behind it. It also had two view finders, one for the 45mm standard lens and one for the 75mm telephoto. Like all German cameras it was well made and had a very solid feel to it. On our holiday in 1952 I persuaded my father to buy me the telephoto lens too.

During my first year at the University I was lucky to obtain some lucrative photographic work, which is historically interesting. It came by courtesy of my very good friend Ben, whose father worked as regional manager for the American Company Western Electric Co. Inc, whose name came up on nearly all films as being responsible for the sound. In 1954 they were pioneering an early 'surround sound' system and many of the suburban Cardiff cinemas were interested in having this fitted. Practically all the small cinemas in the suburbs were owned by the 'Splott Circuit', and I was contracted to visit each with my camera and tripod and take a 180 degree panorama of the interior. Between 4 and 6 pictures were required for each cinema, with 3 different exposure settings for each frame. This was so that the engineers could decide where to fit the speakers without actually having to make the visit to each cinema. For the sake of interest, I am listing all those that I can remember:

The Rialto in Whitchurch, the Monico in Rhiwbina, the Splott in (where else?) Splott, the Gaiety in Roath, the Coloseum in Canton, the Avenue in Ely, the New Cinema in Rumney, the Plaza on North Road, the Tivoli in Llandaff North and the big prize, the Olympia in Cardiff City Centre, which was the head office of the group and its flagship cinema.

It was a bit of a challenge photographically as the only lighting came from the cleaner's lights, which were pretty dim. I think the exposure was minutes rather than seconds, and there was no auto exposure on the camera in those days. My meter did not even give a reading! I then had to go home, develop the films and enlarge all the pictures and stick them together to make the panorama that they had ordered. However with trial and error I did get usable pictures and duly received a cheque for £10 for each cinema that I had to visit. A very useful boost to my meagre bank balance.

During our holidays in Velden, I was very keen to use a camera and, feeling rather guilty, my father handed me the Contax, allowing me to use it as I wished. Unfortunately I cannot find any black and white photos from this period, and guess they must have been lost when we cleared out my mother's house after her death in 1981.

In 1954 I met Jill, and from then on nearly all the pictures I took were of her - and why not? She was a very photogenic subject.

With Jill's best friend Brenda outside the Art College in Greyfriars Road

Jill with Brenda on the Wenallt, Easter Monday 1955

With Lassie, her brother Edward's dog

On the beach at Cold Knap. Note I still had hair.

This and the previous are two of my favourite pictures. These came with me on the "ordeal" that was about to begin

In 1956 the happy and carefree days at university came to an end when I discovered that my name had been omitted from the list of people who had passed their exams, and my National Service deferment had expired. The call-up for National Service came through soon enough, and two wasted years stretched before me. Two events with photographic interest spring to mind. After I had finished my basic training in Bridgnorth, we had to apply for a 'trade' to see us through the remaining 22 months of service. An option was a photographic technician. So I duly applied, and was told to take the test. This involved being ushered into a darkroom, given a handful of old aerial reconnaissance film negatives and asked to make enlargements of them. All straight forward stuff really, but the testers had not told me that the criterion they were looking for was uniformity of the resulting pictures. Unfortunately mine were not good enough, and so I was rejected. To be a Ground Wireless Fitter was my destiny.

Once I had finished the 9 month course, I was posted to Northern Ireland, as has been written about in my two previous volumes. I met up with a fellow enthusiast in Ballykelly called David Harnett, and together we launched an enterprise called Harsch Photographic (HARnett-SCHoenmann), photographers to the troops. It was not a great success, and apart from one photograph of a skiffle group and a picture of me with a guitar, I cannot find any other evidence of our activities. Seeing the results, I can now see why the venture never got anywhere. We did spend a lot of time talking about cameras though.

The pictures that follow are colour slides, which I have copied. Due to the passage of nearly sixty years the quality is pretty awful but I still thought it worth including them, for the sake of historical interest if nothing else.

Our skiffle group featuring Sid, Norman and Jack

A Shackleton aircraft at Ballykelly

An Irish residence near Ballykelly

Chapter 7: early married life in Gloucester

After Jill and I got married in 1959 and settled down to life in Gloucester, it was time to look at photography again. Jill had to run evening classes as part of her job at the College of Art, and I found that they had evening classes in photography too so I duly signed up. I think there were only a small handful of other people interested, but those were less financially strained times and classes ran even if there was only one student. During my time in Cardiff University, I saw an advertisement in the South Wales Echo for a plate camera. Parting with the huge sum of £6 I bought the camera, together with a fitted tripod, leather case and three double-dark slides.

The £6.00 plate camera bought while a student.

I also had bought a huge lens, which was designed for aerial photography, as these were readily available in junk shops at very modest prices. This being soon after the war, very many had found their way onto the market, legally or otherwise. I managed to make an adapter to fit it on the front of the plate camera although it did not boast a shutter. A pill-box lid would have to suffice. We had a young model one evening and I managed to take a very nice picture of her with this outfit. Sad to say in the ensuing 50 years it has been lost. I did take quite a nice colour slide of Jill at the same time with the Akarette and I have found that.

Jill in Gloucester.

Sad to say I have never used the plate camera again but it certainly has increased in value. I swapped the big lens for a smaller one which I will talk about later in Chapter 9.

Chapter 8: a change of camera, the move to Merthyr and the arrival of Julietta

In 1959 I became taken with the idea of a single lens reflex camera, which just happened to coincide with the appearance on the market of the Russian Zenith C. I knew from the camera magazines which I went to the library to read that a company called Johnsons Photopia were the importers and were based in Newcastle under Lyme - this happened to be in the area I covered on my travels as a furniture salesman. The next time I was up there I took the Akarette and telephoto lens to see if I could trade them in. Fortunately they had a Zenith and I was duly impressed. The price was around £30 and this was as much as I could afford to pay. I would really have liked a Contaflex or Retina Reflex which cost nearer £100. They made me a fairly attractive offer for the Akarette and lens and did not ask any awkward questions about its origins. I think the difference I had to pay was about £5 and I came away very happy. 50 years later I still bitterly regret having sold the pair, especially the lens which is now rarer than hen's teeth. What's more, during my 7 years of searching on E-bay I have never found one offered. Such is the folly of youth. The Zenith stayed with me till the mid seventies and was the last of my user cameras that I ever sold. From then on I still kept them all and have meanwhile replaced all the ones that I sold earlier – all except that precious lens….

The Zenith C which I have bought to replace my original.

The camera has an Industar f.3.5/50mm lens, based on the design of the Leitz Elmar, which the Russians had stolen from the Germans as war reparations. The shutter was also copied from the Leica as was the general shape of the body, and also the enormously difficult and awkward film loading arrangement. It was all based on the pre-war Leica 11, which had no slow speeds. The whole thing was built like a tank and primitive in the extreme. To pull the mirror down after taking a picture a piece of cord was used. Instant return mirrors were still many years away. The focusing was a matter of judgement as to when the image appeared sharp as there were no aids like a split image device, as could be found on the Retina and Contaflex. But then you get what you pay for and you can only pay what you can afford. There were no credit cards in those days and hire purchase was a long and complicated process that involved much form filling, credit checks etc, and as I already had the car on hire purchase I did not want any more commitments.

During my period as a travelling furniture salesman, I spent quite a lot of time in Birmingham as that was a thriving industrial city, with a large but not very wealthy population. In addition there was a plethora of small family owned furniture shops who were the sort of customers I was targeting for the cheap and cheerful fireside chairs that I was selling. I think £4.19.6 was the starting price. These shops were on the main arteries out of the city, with names like *Coventry Road, Warwick Road, Stratford Road, Bristol Road* etc. They radiated out like the spokes of a bicycle wheel. Interspersed between these shops were many second-hand or, more accurately, junk shops and as I used to park the car in one location and walk up and down, I had the chance to keep my eye open for bargains. One day while in Acocks Green on the Warwick Road, I chanced on a little shop that had a few cameras in the window. I spotted a Retina1 and thought this would be ideal as a second camera for colour film. After a quick check that everything worked I parted with a week's wages of £2.10.0 and felt enormously pleased with my purchase.

The Retina 1 - Type 148. This is the actual camera I bought 52 years ago. It is the oldest camera that I actually bought for use in the camera collection.

It was not a very wise buy and in truth the camera never got much use. It had a fault with the film-wind mechanism, and sometimes as you wound it did not stop after it had wound on a frame, but went on to wind another frame, leaving a blank space. Now in those days colour film was very expensive indeed, partly because you paid for the processing when you bought the film, and to get back slides with black film was very irksome. You really thought twice before you clicked the shutter with colour film. Also colour film is not very tolerant of incorrect exposures and half a stop either way is critical. When I bought it the camera was more than 20 years old, and I was not convinced the shutter speeds were very accurate. So it ended up in the cupboard, unloved but not forgotten, because in the fullness of time it became the rock on which the camera collection is founded, as will be related in Chapter14. The following pictures are colour slides taken with the Zenith.

In Alexandra Park Penarth, taken probably before our wedding

A harbour in North Wales, taken on our honeymoon

All the upheavals in my working life that followed as the fifties became the sixties has been dealt with in my two previous books, and photography took a back seat for some time until our lives changed on 23rd September 1962 with the arrival of Julietta - in a raging thunderstorm at 5.00 am. Luckily I was asleep in my bed at the time but Jill knew all about it firsthand.

B-Day minus 7, Jill with my parents and grandmother on her last visit to Britain

Julietta at 10 days old.

3 months old

With Auntie Hanna.

Jules and her proud Dad

And beautiful Mum

*Jules with her first camera, and showing great interest
in the Retina Reflex.*

1963 in Bournemouth with Nana on the holiday she funded after selling her house

In 1964 we sold the bungalow in Heolgerrig and moved to the house we had bought in Romilly Road, Canton. Jill's mother contributed to the cost of this as she could no longer manage physically or financially in the family home in Llandough. Jill's father died in 1962 just before Julietta arrived and left no money at all, not even enough for his funeral. All Nana had to live on was her state old age pension, and that was not enough to keep a home going, especially when the inevitable bills started arriving. She tried taking in lodgers to supplement her meagre resources and unfortunately neither her son Edward nor I had any spare money to help. So in the end the sensible thing was to sell her only asset and buy a house together with us big enough for all of us. She had the ground floor and we had the top two floors. It worked very well and she was very happy, her financial problems were solved.

In August 1965, Angelina arrived and completed our family. The system was a bit different back in those days. The first child could be born in hospital, funded by the NHS, but any further children were supposed to be born at home with the help of a midwife. I am afraid neither Jill nor I were happy with that and so we found a private nursing home near Roath Park and that is where Jill went. Angelina was born at about 2.00pm and at that time I was taking Julietta for a walk on the Wenallt. It was a lovely sunny day as I recall. Once again poor Jill had to face the trauma of the birth alone. I always maintained that fathers were only required at the conception and fortunately the matron who was handling the delivery agreed wholeheartedly. Men were just a nuisance and got in the way. My parents, Julietta and I arrived at almost the same time mid afternoon, and Jules spent more time playing with the present of a little cooker that my mother had thoughtfully brought. She did however call her baby sister *Little Lily,* a name that has stuck ever since. Although the 'little' seems to have been dropped.

Angelina taken very soon after she was born 14th August 1965.

Pictures taken by my father

Angelina

Julietta with toilet brush
- one of her favourite toys

Chapter 9: 8mm Cine camera, continental holidays and a Saturday job

About a year after Julietta was born, whilst on a business trip to London I succumbed to the temptation of buying an 8mm cine camera. New models were just beginning to come into the country, with advanced specifications at very tempting prices. One of the more prominent camera shop chains at the time was Bennett's. This chain was bought by Dixon's in 1964 during their period of very rapid growth. The camera itself went under the totally unknown name of Rondo Cinematic Zoom 8.

The Rondo cine camera, and handle.

The camera was clockwork motor driven, had a zoom lens - unusual in 1963 - and a coupled selenium exposure meter, with a needle in the viewfinder that had to be centred for the correct exposure. The lens was f.1.8, did not need to be focused and the zoom range was not given but was usefully big. I cannot remember the price but it was affordable, which was more than could be said about the European cameras that were available at the time. The only other one that I could have bought was the Kodak Brownie which was very basic, and with none of the features of the Rondo (except a recognisable brand name). I am afraid it was the features rather than the name that appealed to me most. To be fair the camera gave faultless service for many years and faithfully recorded the children growing up for many years.

I needed a projector as well and at the time there was a company in South London called Headquarters and General Supplies who were big on advertising, with whole page adverts in the papers every week. They offered a projector at a very low price with quite an advanced specification. At that time all that the camera shops had to offer was from the top European brands at prices that were completely out of my reach. The Rexina 8 which I bought from them obviously came from Japan and to my mind the quality was top notch. It had a zoom lens too, which was useful when using it in different rooms, and gave the ability to fill the screen with the projector quite close to it. On one of our trips to London - and we did go quite often back then to visit friends - I called in to their shop and bought one.

Soon afterwards I bought a Haynorama Editor which was essential for joining films and cutting out the bad bits.

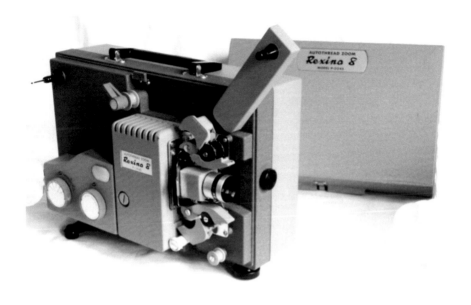

The projector, and editor shown below.

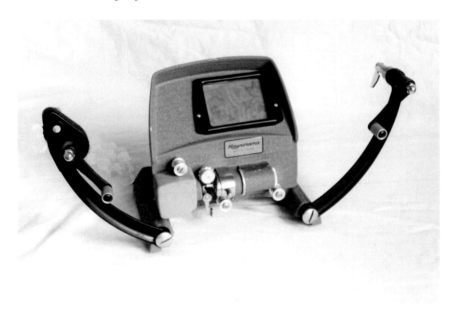

In 1964, a year before the arrival of Angelina, Jill and I decided that we really deserved a holiday, so my parents bravely offered to have Julietta for the three weeks that we planned to be away. She was less than 2 years old and must have been a bit of a handful for them for such a long period. Looking back, I just do not know how they coped. I was very much into cine at that time and there is a fairly lengthy film of our journey, but very few photographs. Perhaps there were more, but they do not appear to have survived the house moves and occasional clear outs. The only ones I can find Jill kept in a polythene bag in her workroom, and have already been published in my second volume under the heading of 'The Rapier'. I think the reason for the paucity of photographs is that carrying both a cine camera and an SLR is a bit much: taking pictures with either was a much more laborious process than it is now, and so it became a case of one or the other. The cine camera seems to have won most of the time.

The Sunbeam Rapier in Germany, 1964

When we came back and went to collect Julietta, we were staggered to find she did not recognise us and was a bit reluctant to come home. As we left, my poor father was still trying to remove her artistic efforts with a crayon from his walls. She was quite proud of her handiwork too.

The sixties was a very busy period for me, with very little time for hobbies. I changed jobs every two years, got very involved with the car club, and spent three nights a week taxi driving. In 1970 we had our first big holiday as a family when we drove to Millstadt in Austria. Once again there is plenty of 8mm cine but very few photographs. I am indeed indebted to Jill that she kept a few of them squirreled away at the back of a cupboard as whatever I kept has been lost. I think a few of these deserve to be included as it was a memorable holiday, more so than many much more ambitious journeys that we undertook in the ensuing years. We had worked so hard to afford it and the sun seemed to shine for most of the time, and so we were extremely happy.

1970, on holiday in Millstadt in Austria.

Millstadt 1970

Either just before or just after this holiday, I decided to give up my evening job taxi-driving. After the murder threat and the night on the roof, and being under great pressure from both Jill and my mother, I decided that enough was enough, and called it a day - or night, to be more accurate. Also I had not long before started my new job at Controller Contacts and in 1971 was given a company car. Having to only bear the running cost of one car privately did ease the strain on my finances considerably.

In 1974, I was tempted to buy a second camera, mainly because of the limitations of only having one camera, and wanting to use not only black and white film but also colour slide film. It always seemed to happen that you had the wrong film loaded in the camera. Just at this time Russian cameras were coming onto the market, and I thought a Kiev 4 would be ideal. The history behind this camera is interesting. The original design was from Carl Zeiss in Jena near Dresden and was sold pre-war as the Contax 111. Very similar to the Contax 11 that my father bought just after the war and which I was allowed to use during our holidays in Velden.

The Kiev 4, this is the actual camera, but the telephoto lens and finder are later purchases.

After the bombing of Dresden in the last few months of the war the factory was badly damaged, but when the Russians arrived they took everything they could find back to Russia as war reparations. They stashed away all the machinery, tools and drawings on several trains back to Kiev, where the old Arsenal was converted to make cameras. Not surprisingly the German staff decided not to go to Russia, and instead set up a new factory near Stuttgart under the name of Zeiss Ikon. There were protracted legal battles about the name, and in the end the Russians could not use the Contax or Zeiss names, which is why the cameras were called Kiev.

They did a similar trick with Leica, although they could not take the tooling. As Wetzlar was in the Western region, they just stole the designs of the Leica 11, made identical copies and sold them as Feds and Zorkis. The picture also shows the 13.5cm f.4.0 telephoto lens and multi-lens finder which they copied and made; I was fortunate enough to acquire these many years later for my collection.

I do not think the camera has had more than 2 films through it, as the results were not very good and I am printing two slides that were definitely taken with the camera. I say this because I am pictured holding the Zenith (see next page), so it is only the Kiev that could have taken the pictures. My powers of detection and deduction are still quite good. It also proved to be a bit cumbersome carrying two cameras, and usually the opportunity to take a picture did not last very long - it was not long enough to take the scene or subject twice. Especially not the children as the perfect moment is only fleeting. The camera cost about £45 and I still have it today, literally 'as new'. It is still worth about the same and there are hundreds of them around. A Contax 111 though is worth about £250. The quality of the Kiev was not great as the accuracy of manufacturing was nowhere near as good as it was in Germany, and the cameras were assembled by unskilled (and often unwilling) workers. The lens on mine for instance definitely wobbles and when I mentioned this to the shop owner, he assured me that *they all do that*. Perhaps that was why it never got used very much.

This picture must have been taken with the Kiev, because I am holding the Zenith. It is probably on Lake Windermere.

Probably another Kiev picture, but I am not sure.

A distinct downside of the Zenith was that although it had an interchangeable lens with a 39mm Leica thread, the extra space required for the reflex mirror meant that Leica lenses did not fit. However Leica accessories did and I managed to buy a set of extension tubes from what is now the Camera Centre in Cardiff and a bellows close-focusing device, with 39mm threads. I also swapped my old aircraft lens for a small lens and shutter unit from an old roll-film camera which was an f.4.8/135mm Ennatar Anastigmat and fixed this to a short extension tube with 'Loy plastic metal', so fashioning myself a telephoto lens with the bellows between the lens and the camera body.

The old Ennar lens which became my telephoto.

It was not very elegant, and definitely very cumbersome to use. I do not consider it one of my greatest achievements. I was also keen to make a slide copier unit, as there was not any easy method of getting prints from colour slides. There was a process called Cibachrome which was not only very expensive but also incredibly slow, and if you made one print in a night that was good going. It also required colour print chemicals and special tanks, none of which did I have. So I devised a rig made of wood, with a paint tin containing a 100 watt lamp and a slide holder at the business end It also had a mount for the camera fitted with the bellows housing and the camera's own 50mm lens, close to the slide. This gave a 1:1 magnification and the camera was mounted quite close to the slide. The old paint tin became exceptionally hot as I recall and due to the strong smell of burning paint it was best to work in the open air. The results were in fact not too bad, especially on black and white film. Using colour print film was not so good though as my 100 watt bulb gave everything a very yellow cast. When I finally sold the camera (co-incidentally to the Camera Centre) I sold the bellows housing too. On reflection I wish that I had kept both, but I needed the money to fund a new camera (which will be dealt with in the next chapter). Although my contraption lived in the attic for many years, it eventually ended up in the skip which was really the proper place for it.

I think it was in 1975 that we were suffering from a more severe cash crisis than usual and I once again felt that I had to earn some extra money to supplement my not very generous pay from Controller Contacts Ltd. This was the time of the 'three day week' and Ted Heath's disastrous spell as Prime Minister with inflation in double figures. We were having pay rises twice a year, but they were never really enough to cover our out-goings. Taxi driving was not an option and so I resorted to the local paper to see what was on offer. One thing that came up was a local photographic studio that specialized in weddings, wanting photographers to attend weddings and use their own cameras to take informal pictures. The studio, run by David Mathias, would supply the films, handle all the processing and pay a few pounds for a day's work, usually on a Saturday. They would not pay for the first attempt as this was essentially a trial run. I duly turned up at a church in Crwys Road and have to admit that I was completely out of my depth. I did not have an electronic flash unit as this was still very expensive, and my cheap Russian camera was not up to the job of taking pictures with 'available light'. So I handed in my two rolls of film and it was no surprise that I never heard from them again.

Back to the South Wales Echo and I saw another advertisement from Dixons looking for Saturday staff in the photographic department. I went for the interview, seemed to click with Sheila the manageress and got the job. The pay was £6 per day cash in hand. This of course equates to £10, as far as gross wages go and I was quite happy to accept it. There was also the incentive of 25% discount on purchases. The shop was on Queen Street, opposite M&S and the Midland (now HSBC)

Bank. I worked with very pleasant people one of whom, Steve, I still see to this day as he is now the manager of Jacobs Cameras in High Street. At that time Dixons was *the* major force in photographic retailing (in the provinces at least) having bought out or seen off most of the competition. Most of the cameras they sold were their own brands which had little kudos among knowledgeable amateurs, but these were not among the clientele who shopped there. Their main 'quality' brand was Chinon which was sold exclusively by them: some of their cameras were very well specified and well made, but still relatively pricey. Their other 'budget' brand was Prinz and many common cameras were badged with this name. Dixons was great at offering instant credit HP terms, requiring nothing more than some ID from the customer and a lot of form-filling by the sales staff, then a nod from the manager. Although they took credit cards, these were not as universal as they are now and often people paid cash. In those days Dixons sold no white goods at all and were only just getting going with televisions. This was long before the days of CDs, DVDs and even VCRs. They sold radios, cassette players, binoculars and also cameras, lenses, enlargers and film. They did film processing too of course. I must say I did enjoy my time there: the shop was always crowded, the customers mostly good natured and pleased with what they bought. Cardiff was nearly always at the top of their 'league' table for stores outside London.

We had to patiently explain the basics of photography to some, especially those who wanted something more than just a point-and-shoot camera. We sold the Russian Zenith cameras (which had progressed a little further from the one I still had) and were an ideal camera for students and beginners. They also offered the East German Praktica cameras, which were more stylish and sophisticated than the rather basic and grim Russian products but were somewhat prone to going wrong. This led to one of the real downsides of the job - the warrantee claims and the repairs. Dixons did not have a policy of giving money back, or giving replacements for items that failed during the warrantee period. Instead they would send them away to their own repair shop to try to fix them.

Although parts of the Dixon Empire were extremely efficient, the repair department was not one of them. Customers would bring their faulty stuff back and we would cheerfully take it in, write out all the forms and tell them to call back in 10 or 14 days. It would then be taken upstairs and put on a table to join the hundreds of others that were already there, and some had been there for a few weeks already. Eventually they would be sent off where they would stay at the repair shop for weeks or months longer. Meanwhile the increasingly irate customers would come in every fortnight to be fobbed off with more and more excuses. All this was before the days of consumer watchdogs and television programs highlighting the failures of the shop and system. Perhaps some things like service have changed for the better, as well as electronic products becoming more and more reliable. How often do things go wrong nowadays? Practically never! It was not like that in 1975 when often it did not even work on taking it out of the box.

One new innovation that we sold was electronic calculators and Sinclair was the big name at the time. These items were just becoming affordable, albeit still fairly expensive. They still had red LED screens and a voracious appetite for batteries. The better ones could actually multiply and the even better ones had a memory. Demonstrating these to people who had never seen one before made you feel like Einstein or a magician at least. We totally take them for granted today but then it was a revelation. My other abiding memory is the music that played continually, and Barry White's "Love's Theme" brings back memories of my time behind the counter whenever I hear it.

I stayed there for about 2 years and have quite fond memories of the time spent there, considering it all part of life's rich experiences.

Chapter 10: new cameras, evening classes and a memorable holiday

In 1978 I felt that the time had come to invest in a new and more up-to-date camera. Things had moved on a lot since buying the Zenith in the late fifties and it was now approaching its 20th birthday, but still working well. Having seen during my time at Dixon's what was available, my appetite was wetted. The trouble was that I still had only limited funds so the problem was what to buy. I had left Dixons by then, so the 25% discount that I could have had was no longer on offer. I decided that I could only afford £80-£100 and definitely wanted a new single lens reflex with the best specification for the money. I ruled out the cheaper offerings from Dixons and also all the East German Prakticas - I knew all about the problems of unreliability - and thought the best bet was something made in Japan. There were really only two readily available with very similar specifications: the Petri and the Carena. In the end I liked the look of the latter and there was a dealer selling them, called F.W.Haines (Photomarkets) in Swansea. On my next sales trip I stopped there to look at it and felt it was what I wanted.

The Carena SRH 1001

The camera is now very rare although not in a valuable way, but because very few were sold. Its origin is not quite clear but research shows that the name was used by a Swiss importer, who supplied a chain in Germany called Photo Porst and they had a brand name - Carena. I feel therefore that these were imported to Britain in small quantities by a very limited number of shops. It is generally accepted that it was made by Cosina who are well known for making products that others can badge as their own. The camera has all the usual features that were available at the time: Cds (Cadmium di-sulphide) through-the-lens metering, operated by pressing a button on the side of the lens housing. The shutter speed is set as required, then the button pressed and the aperture ring turned until the needle in the viewfinder is centred. The main feature that the camera lacked was a split-image rangefinder, but it had a microprism arrangement instead which worked quite well. It had an f1.8/50mm lens and focal plane shutter. I sold the Zenith and all the bits and pieces I had accumulated to Camera Centre in Cardiff and was only poorer by about £50.

Very soon after this purchase and fired up with enthusiasm, I signed up for a photography class in Whitchurch. There was logic in this as Jill was already attending classes in upholstery in the same location, and as they were on the same night it made sense to go together. It turned out that the main interest was in 'glamour' photography, but we also did some processing work as all the facilities were there. The school was exceedingly well equipped as Whitchurch was one of the flagship schools in Cardiff. Colour printing was just becoming popular although the process never really appealed to me. It is very slow and involves a rotating drum with just a small amount of liquid and several changes of chemicals before a picture emerges about an hour later. As the paper was fairly expensive it was necessary to make a test strip first, and so to produce one picture it took at least 2 hours. Luckily commercial laboratories had machines for this and using a postal service like Bonusprint meant that 36 prints could be done for under £3 and in about 3 days too. We also made prints from colour slides using the Cibachrome process, but that was even more complicated and took even longer. I produced only one print ever, and was quite proud of it. Unfortunately, I can no longer find it….

Our glamour photo set-up was very impressive. We had coloured backgrounds in several shades which came as rolls of thick paper with a stand to hold them. We had 3 Bowen Studio flash lights which had tungsten modelling lights built into them, so that the lighting effect could be assessed before the actual picture was taken. We could never have imagined back then that the day would come when you can take a picture and a split-second later see the result on the screen on the back of the camera. Back then you pressed the button and hoped you had got the settings right. We did have flash meters which were held in front of the subject and the flash fired, which then gave you an exposure setting. The lights were triggered by slave units built into them, but there was only one lead coming from the nearest flash unit and so only one person could take a picture at one time. The poor girls really earned their money by having to hold a pose and keep smiling while 15 of us took pictures in turn. Some of the chat-up lines were interesting too, but did keep them smiling. Not that I was ever any good at that sort of thing and the smiles I got were out of sympathy.

There was quite a lot of 'camera snobbery' too, based on what you had hanging around your neck. Top of the heap were those really dedicated photographers who eschewed 35mm, and could afford Hasselblads. Slightly below them came Bronicas and Mamiya 6X6 single lens reflexes. Next in the pecking order came top level 35mm SLRs like the Canon A-1. Then came the third division cameras like Canon's AE-1, Olympus OM 1 and OM2, Minolta and Pentax,. Very far behind all of these came the non-league efforts like my Carena! Sad really, but that is life. I bought an f2.8/135mm Hanimex telephoto lens for not very much money, and this was viewed with the same disdain as the camera, but was a useful lens for head and shoulder close-ups. It was good enough for the not-very-wonderful pictures that I managed to turn out. The old saying is that it's the man behind the camera that counts, not the actual camera, when it comes to getting results. I am including some of the work I did (see below) to show that my time was not totally wasted. All of the following pictures were taken with the Carena or Canon A1. I cannot be sure which is which.

110

111

114

We went out taking night shots in Cardiff city centre and in the spring, daytime outings to the Castle Grounds. On one night our tutor and mentor Bryn Williams announced
"Tonight we have a topless model..............................

We had a full class that evening and no mistake. When the pictures came back from the processing lab, I thought it best not to show them to Jill.....suspecting she may not have understood as wives often don't. So I put them right at the bottom of the drawer in my writing desk and forgot all about them. Many months, possibly years later, I came home from work and found them prominently displayed on the top of the desk. I wonder what she had been looking for to actually find them. She never told me and from then on the class was always referred to rather disparagingly as *the pornography class*. The pictures got torn up in disgust but my trawl through the old photographs has found that one has survived and rather shame-facedly I am including it with the selection.

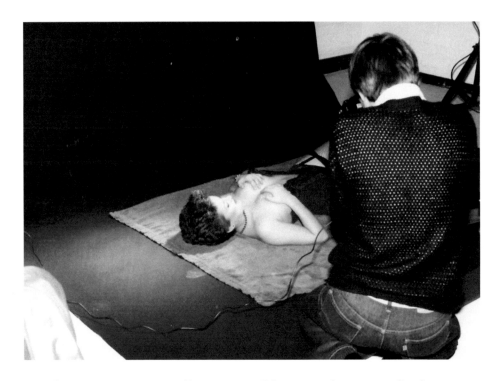

There are no more guilty secrets. I have made my confession, hopefully to great relief all round.

In 1979 I thought we could afford a continental holiday as we had not had one since 1970, and both of the other holidays we had taken since then had been in Scotland - one in Dingwall in 1974 and then Lochgilphead in 1976. Both of these had been working holidays, with Jill and the girls staying in a cottage and me heading off to make customer visits around Glasgow and Edinburgh. We also did the Newcastle and Middlesbrough calls on the way down.

I thought in 1979 that we could do something similar with calls in Holland, and Germany, have a fortnight's holiday in Austria and then make calls in Strasbourg and Paris on the way back. Luckily Controller Contacts would pick up the bills for the car ferry, fuel, tolls and hotels; all I needed to pay was for the hire of the apartment. The journey has been written about in both my previous books as the year 1979 has a special significance in my life story. I think in this volume I need only cover the photographic aspect. I took the Carena and used mainly colour slides though as I only had one camera, cannot find any prints taken on that holiday. The slides show pictures from the whole route we took and so I assume that there are no prints. I do not think I took any cine films either as my interest had waned with the very poor results the 8mm gave in those days. Much better video cameras were just around the corner, but I did not know that at the time. What follows is a selection from the slides:

Amsterdam

The Rhine near Singen

Salzburg viewed from the castle which overlooks the town

The house in which we stayed in Velden. We had the ground floor

The Worthersee on which Velden lies

Rural Austrian scene

The Opera in Paris

My lovely girls in front of Notre Dame, Paris

There was another photographic venture which deserves mention at this point. In 1980 Jill was working very hard with her fashion business, had hit on the idea of making dresses, skirts, tops and coats out of suede, and wanted to publicise the fact that she could offer these items. She made up a range and we discussed the idea with a firm of printers run by the Scaglionis who we knew through the children, as they all went to the same school. We got a photogenic daughter (Carys) of another friend to model and Angelina was conscripted too. All the pictures were taken in Michelstone woods, and the trees and bushes served as a changing room. The results are shown on the next page.

⑤ Pretty slim-fit skirt with inset godets which fluke out at the bottom.

⑥ Charming waist-tied blouse which marries up with Style 5.

⑦ Simple slip of a dress which can be worn also as a pinafore. Has own self tie belt.

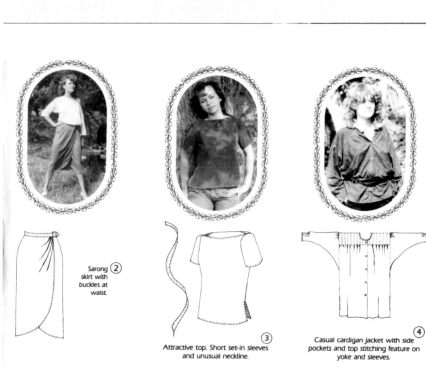

Sarong ② skirt with buckles at waist.

③ Attractive top. Short set-in sleeves and unusual neckline.

④ Casual cardigan jacket with side pockets and top stitching feature on yoke and sleeves.

Chapter 11: start of the Electrical Spare Parts era in 1979

The last two months of 1979 were a traumatic experience for me as has been well documented in my two earlier books. Christmas and New Year's Eve especially so, with the clinking of many glasses and toasts of 'cheers' to a very uncertain future, when I alone would be in control of my fate. As this book deals primarily with photography, I have to say that the camera played a large part in the success story that followed in the ensuing 24 years.

I knew that success depended on building a personal relationship with customers. In order to have something to refer to when I was not with them and they needed a part, I had to have a leaflet to leave with them. However I needed this in a hurry as I wanted to make visits as soon as possible in the January of 1980. At that time, my thinking was to have a general brochure showing what I could offer together with a price list of the parts I held in stock. I would have to get the brochure properly printed, but the price lists I could run off on a duplicator which I still happened to have. This actually belonged to the SWAC car club, and even though I had resigned as secretary they did not want it back. I had two problems with the photography. On the one hand I did not have the funds to have it done professionally and would have to do it myself; on the other hand I didn't at that time have delivery of the stock that I planned to sell. I did though have a briefcase full of samples that had accompanied me on my travels for Controller Contacts and had somehow left with me when I was expelled from my office. These would have to suffice.

I also did not have much of a clue how to take the pictures and discussed it with Bryn our evening class teacher. I wanted to avoid the shadows that came with flash guns or flood lights, and I only had access to a very small cheap flash gun. He suggested putting the contacts on a sheet of glass which was supported by two chairs with a piece of white paper on the floor beneath. This did seem to achieve the desired effect so I presented the results to the firm of printers and they seemed to be satisfied that they could use them. There were also many items that I wanted to sell which I did not have at the time, and so they managed to take pictures from the supplier's catalogues and reproduce them. Shamefully I think I forgot to ask permission, but time was of the essence and the catalogues were American so perhaps it was worth the risk. Hard as I have tried, I cannot find one of these catalogues anymore and so cannot reproduce one here. To be truthful I was not very proud of them but they lasted for the next 2 years.

After the sad death of my mother right on the last day of 1980 we had the task of sorting out her affairs and disposing of her household. The task of sorting it all fell on Helly, Alan and me, with Helly and Alan doing the lion's share of the work. I had a one-year-old business to keep going virtually single-handed and could only spare a limited amount of time. In the end everything was settled, the house and contents sold and the proceeds were shared between us. Jill said to me that I should treat myself to a 'decent' camera and as this time there was not a serious cost constraint, I bought a Canon A1 - the very pinnacle of what was available at the time. It put me in the first division of 35mm users at the photography class too which was a side benefit.

The A1 was a fully automatic camera with manual features, so was very flexible in use. It had the all-important split image rangefinder function and programmed exposure modes. I was really thrilled with it and it would prove invaluable when it came to taking the photographs for future catalogues.

The Canon A1

The next major event came in 1982 when it became necessary to move the business out of our home and find a factory unit. Luckily this was happening just when the country was emerging from the grim, strife-filled period that epitomised the Wilson-Callaghan years: business optimism was just beginning to return and new buildings were going up everywhere. A friend of mine was developing a new estate of factory units on the former Dowlais steelworks site on East Moors Road in Cardiff and I took one that was nearly ready for occupation. Another significant event was that we had to buy a computer and use it to run the business. This seemed like the ideal time to create a stock numbering system which would be the key to the whole business, all based on the new catalogue which I had planned. The catalogue would be split according to the type of items we sold. Contacts were the bed-rock of the business so they came first, then battery plugs, fuses carbon brushes etc. I took the pictures on the floor of my office, laying the parts out on a white background.

For lighting, I still needed to avoid shadows so used a single large flash gun firing upwards into a large white umbrella and a flash meter to determine the exposure. In these pre-digital days,

I needed to take the films to be processed before seeing the results and being sure that I had everything right.

The first working catalogue was produced in 1982:

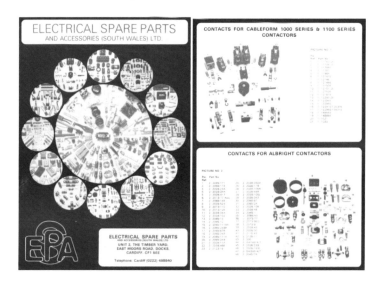

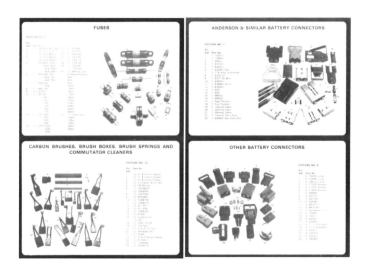

The next catalogue came in 1985 when we moved to Unit 6:

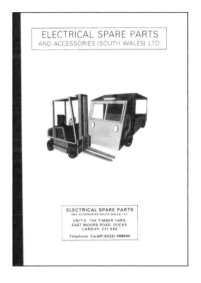

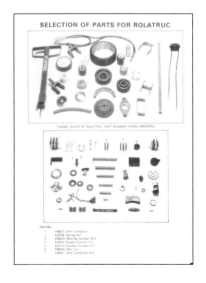

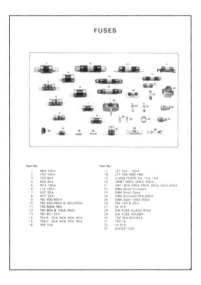

The final catalogue came in the mid-nineties and was cream coloured. There was an earlier one - in blue - produced in about 1990, but I can no longer find a copy. It was very similar to the yellow version (shown below) in its final format with four pictures per page, but contained less items on each as we were still growing fast. A pity there is not one left but that's life!

This catalogue was reprinted several times and thousands of copies went out all over the country. It is safe to say that just about every fork-truck engineer had one in his van and they were our best-selling tool ever. As new products came into the range we produced extra leaflets but luckily the business was such that once the correct formula was discovered there was no need to change much. If for instance we took on a new line of seats we produced a leaflet devoted to those.

The photography aspect was a long and tedious process. I invested in a piece of light yellow cloth which was laid out on the floor of my office. We then collected all the parts for each picture from the stores and Angelina carefully and painstakingly laid them out in as artistic a pattern as possible. Each page consisted of four pictures and I used two cameras - one loaded with colour slide film and the other with colour print film. The printers wanted to work with the slide transparencies and we needed the prints to make working dummy catalogues for numbering, while also composing the text that accompanied each page. The text was a description of each part shown and was an enormous amount of work, but paid handsome dividends. One company in Europe reproduced it illegally in black and white, reprinting the text in French which caused a bit of friction: I do not think their business lasted very long.

Our main competitor Machine Electrics, who later bought the business, produced a very similar catalogue and I felt that imitation is the sincerest form of flattery. I am pleased to say though they made a very basic error which they bitterly regretted ever after. We had deliberately chosen the pale yellow background colour which allowed copies of the page to be sent by fax, the chief means of communication at the time. Machine Electrics chose a turquoise background which looked stunning as a picture but came through the fax as deep black….and totally useless. It certainly stopped people making pirate copies though which could have been their primary concern.

The catalogue of 1982 was taken with the A1 and the standard f1.8/50mm lens that came with the camera. The fact that there were not that many items on each picture meant that it was adequate. But by the time we came to do the third catalogue in 1985 I thought that a wide angle lens would be more use. So I bought a Tamron f3.5/28-70 zoom lens. This made it much easier to fill the frame without having to be too far away from the subject and requiring too large an aperture. Sometime later I had convinced myself that I needed a telephoto lens and bought a Tamron f3.5/35-210. On reflection, this was not one of my best ideas. The lens is made of metal and very heavy; it has a 'trombone' action; when it is fitted to the camera and carried on the shoulder, the heavy front end extends to its full reach and becomes extremely cumbersome.

Batteries were also a bit of a problem. I was using a Vivitar 285 as the main flash at full power, firing upwards into the umbrella, and took three exposures at varying apertures with each camera. I was using rechargeable batteries and after several recharging cycles these had trouble holding their charge. So 24 flashes were needed to take one page with 4 pictures on each page and we were lucky if one set of batteries sufficed. We would then leave them to charge overnight,

Canon fit Tamron FD lenses

In 1985 Canon announced the EOS range and the first camera to be offered was the EOS650. By 1987 ESP&A as a company was doing pretty well and making good profits. I had a good relationship with our accountants and they agreed that there was no reason why the company could not buy a new camera to take the pictures for the catalogues which were the key to the whole business. So as soon as these new autofocus cameras came onto the market, I hot-footed down to the shops to try one. Camera Centre in the Morgan Arcade had one and it took me very few minutes to agree the price. There was no haggling in those days except for a tour of the three outlets in Cardiff to see who was cheapest. But the cameras were so new that everyone was offering them at the same price and the final decider was the offer of a free filter. Of course today it is easier to compare prices on the Internet, but that was still a long way off. I bought the camera with the 'kit' lens which was an f3.5/35-70 zoom. I felt this would cover all the needs for the catalogues as well as holidays. The camera had all the features that the A1 had as far as programs and metering goes and the autofocus and metering were a delight to use. How did we ever manage without them? If you want to find out what a boon it is try using an old camera with a rangefinder.

In the same year I bought Jill an Olympus AF1 as I had been seduced by their advertising, which featured such luminaries as David Bailey and Lord Lichfield. This was a fully automatic point and shoot camera with auto focus and exposure and I thought it would be just the job for her. It had a top quality Zuiko f3.5/35 lens and was small and handy compared with 35mm SLRs. I do not think it got too much use though as mostly on holidays I took pretty well everything worth taking and it seemed pointless to take the same scenes twice. Jill only got more interested with the arrival of digital and the possibility of seeing the results instantly. I have always liked Olympus compacts though and stuck with them for a long time.

133

The EOS 650

The Olympus AF-1

These two cameras came with us on our round the world tour in 1990 and served us well with many photographs that still adorn our walls. I am including a few samples below but there are many more and it was hard to make a choice:

The street market in Guangzhou where we got well and truly lost

Hong Kong Island taken from Kowloon

Melbourne by night, taken from our bedroom window

Fast asleep in Sidney Zoo

Jill, taken in the evening in the dining room of the Fijian Resort

The Queen Mary in Long Beach, California

137

A dalliance with video cameras:

For Christmas in 1992 Jill bought me a video camera which came as a big surprise, especially as I knew how much they cost at the time with very little change out of £1000. Jill is always generous to a fault. The camera was a Sanyo and came with all the usual features of the time. It had a zoom lens which had autofocus, it had an electronic black and white view finder which was seen through a longish tube. This was all before the days of foldout LCD screens. It used a cassette a little smaller than audio cassettes and used both sides of the tape, with each side lasting about 30 minutes. Unfortunately the battery which came with the camera lasted for about 15 minutes and so it was not long before I was back looking around the camera shops for the heavy duty version. This cost another £100 but did last about an hour. The camera could then be used as a video player and the output taken to a television, or recorded onto VHS cassettes and played back at will. I enjoyed using it and it came with us on all our subsequent holidays, but I always had trouble persuading anyone to watch my efforts. The pictures taken during the QE 2's departure from New York with the seven blasts from the siren still make Angelina and Andy shudder. This scene comes up on each of the six occasions that we went on that ship. The only picture I have of this camera is shown on page 154.

In 1998 when our grand-daughter Clara was born, I thought that the arrival of the next generation deserved some better equipment. This coincided with the appearance of digital video cameras and so I bought myself a state-of-the-art Panasonic unit. This still used miniature tape cassettes as the advent of hard-disk recorders was still 10 years away. The camera was a huge step forward from the Sanyo both as regards size and weight, but also ease of use. It had an early form of image-stabilization and a 10X zoom range.

It was of course auto-everything too. It had a foldout viewing screen as well as a colour electronic viewfinder and was a neat gadget as can be seen in the picture below:

The Panasonic digital video camera.

Otherwise it worked the same way as the Sanyo with the output being transferred onto VHS tapes. Luckily I still have two VCR machines but one day I may have to copy them all to DVDs. The only question is, will the DVD format last much longer than the VHS tapes or will they both become obsolete before too long? At around this time I saw an advertisement for a gadget to enable one to copy 8mm films onto a video camera and then on to VHS tape. I thought this would be useful to keep all my old films of our own children's childhood. The projector I had bought in London more than 40 years earlier was still working and so I set up the equipment on the dining room table.

The principle was that the projector was pointed at the gadget from a distance of about 6 inches and the beam of light hit a mirror, which played the image on a ground glass screen on another side of the box. The video camera was then set up to record the image on the screen and by starting both simultaneously, a copy would be made. It worked well in theory but not really very successfully in practice. The projector was really noisy and as there was no way (that I could discover anyway) of recording without sound the racket on playback was awful. The only way to watch the results was with the television muted but that did not seem right either. Another big drawback was that the pictures were not evenly illuminated, having a very bright hot-spot of light right in the middle. I copied my father's Brazilian film and a few of my own, but then disaster struck and the drive belt of the projector broke. Sadly I was not skilled enough to dismantle the whole thing to replace it. The design is such that it requires a complete strip down to do a simple job like replacing a frail rubber belt. Sometime later I still felt that these old films should be viewable and so I found a firm in London which offered to copy 8mm films onto VHS tape. The price was pretty steep - something like £10 for a 5 minute roll - but I still sent off all my films. What came back was very disappointing indeed. I think it had been done on the same gadget although they had managed to eliminate the noise. The hotspot was also there to some extent, but what made them unviewable was that only 80% of the picture was recorded: whenever people were in the picture their heads were missing. When I complained, I was told that this was the only way they could do them and I was stuck with them. And *No, I couldn't have a refund.* I thought of a few rude names for the company and put it down to experience.

A very short time ago I was at a camera club meeting and on one of the sales tables a chap was offering a Sekonic 8mm projector in full working order for the very reasonable price of

£6.00. Further he had a notice saying that the price would halve at noon. So I waited till 12.01 pm and bought it for £3.00. So I now have a working projector, but still no audience for my film shows. Perhaps when they are as old as I am they may want to see them again. Who knows?

The unsuccessful film copying gadget

My £3.00 film projector

Chapter 12: more new Canons and a move to compacts

In 1993 Canon introduced the EOS 100 onto the market and I thought it was time to push the boat out again. We were already planning a new catalogue so I thought the cost was justified. What's more the EOS 100 introduced some interesting new features which I thought would be of use to me. It had a new belt drive system for the film transport and shutter wind which was much quieter and faster than before. The camera was also available with USM lenses which also focused faster and with less noise. I also wanted a bigger zoom range and so bought the camera with an f4.0/35-135 lens.

The Canon EOS 100

The camera in the picture above is shown with a 28-80mm lens which came as a kit with the EOS 50E bought later. I still have the camera but unfortunately it suffers from a problem which is quite common to Canons of that era: the plastic material covering the body exudes a sticky substance which must be the polymer leaching out. There is no known cure except to peel the material off and re-cover the camera. To have it done professionally is not cost effective as these cameras have no real value either for a user or for a collector. Very recently I have been able to replace the camera at very little cost for an example which does not have this problem. As far as I can remember the camera only came on one holiday when we went to the West Coast of America in 1993.

Captain Marvel exiting his cannon at Universal Studios

Taken from the highest point overlooking San Francisco

We found that the ship on the left sailed from Penarth on its last voyage

145

Picture taken in Picton Ontario with John and Ann Cape. John was my best friend in school and sadly died in 2010

An atmospheric picture of Columbia University in Manhattan

Picture taken in Forest Hills NY with Gusti and Emil Glauber,
both of whom lived to be over 100 but have sadly passed on

The following year we went on a memorable holiday to New
Orleans after our usual business trip which I think started with
a flight to Montreal, then a drive to Toronto with a visit to my
friend the late John Cape in between. From Toronto we flew to
Chicago, then to Kansas City in Missouri and then onto
Memphis, before finally flying to New Orleans. Who says
business is not hard work? Before going I thought that we
needed to cut down on the amount we had to carry as hand
luggage. The answer seemed to be in buying a high quality
compact camera and leave the SLRs at home. I was still taking
the JVC video camera which caused my one shoulder to droop
significantly. Wanting to remain faithful to Olympus, I thought
their recently introduced Superzoom 110 would fit the bill:

A replacement for the stolen Olympus Superzoom 110.

This camera has autofocus and exposure, built in flash and a zoom lens 38-110mm which was quite unusual at the time. It was quite expensive too, costing around £260. Unfortunately the camera was not to last very long as it was stolen in Lafayette from the boot of the hire car we were using. My own stupid fault really. We stayed in a motel on the edge of town and when I unloaded the luggage from the boot the camera was right at the back; as I knew I would not need it till next day I left it there. Next morning of course there was no sign of the camera and a lot of cursing from me. I did not think much of Lafayette before and even less afterwards. We still had a week of the holiday left and so we went round the camera shops in New Orleans to see what we could buy. I did not want to spend a large amount and the staff were all particularly unhelpful when they discovered this. They were intent on selling me one of their range of digital compacts which were just starting to appear, and which I had never even seen before. So in the end we went to Wal-Mart and I found a Nikon Fun-Touch 5. This looked quite a well specified camera for $19.95, with auto focus, exposure and a 29mm Nikon lens - I thought that being a Nikon it must be OK. But the proof of the pudding is in the eating, and the results, though usable, fell a long way short of the quality of the Olympus.

The Nikon Fun-Touch 5 bought in Wal-Mart in New Orleans, Louisiana

The first three pictures are taken with the Olympus and the last two with the Nikon.

The Toronto skyline taken from a ferry to an island nearby

The French Quarter in New Orleans. We ate on the balcony of the restaurant shown

The floating Casino at Natchez. The whole thing is a modern construction and totally fake

Below are just two of the pictures taken with the Nikon:

A view that has gone forever

Dining on the Queen Elizabeth 2 on the journey home .

Canon Z135 compact and EOS 50E - the last of the film cameras

Soon after our return from the New Orleans holiday I wanted to replace the stolen compact camera, as I was really taken with their ease of use, versatility, and ever improving specifications. Julietta had asked for a new camera for her birthday, and I had bought her a Canon Z135, which she found to be very useful. So within a month or two, I was back in the same shop buying a second one for myself.

The Canon Z135.

The camera was fully automatic as regards focusing and exposure, and had a very good zoom range from 38mm to 135mm. On the back was Canon's familiar control dial giving a selection of program modes such as, spot metering, and settings for sport, night time, portrait and macro. There are also buttons for the self-timer, forced flash, red-eye reduction, and mid-roll rewind. All in all it was a very sophisticated camera for a compact, even if it was no great beauty to behold. It cost £150, and served me well for many years until the arrival of the digital age. In 1996 we went to Maui in Hawaii, and in 1998 to Yellowstone National Park. I took the Sanyo video camera as well, which I thought gave me enough to carry. Luckily the airlines were not as strict then regarding hand luggage.

Jill with the Subaru Legacy Outback, the only good car we ever had in America. In the background are the chalets, one of which we had at the Yellowstone Hotel

The Grand Teton Mountain range between Yellowstone Park and Jackson Hole

*The Grand Canyon of the Yellowstone River, the falls, and me
with video camera*

As we were leaving New York on the QE2, black clouds rolled in from the east and the sky went black. The sun which was low in the west still shone and lit up the buildings in spectacular fashion. Minutes later there was a deluge and thunderstorm and all the camera enthusiasts fled below to escape a soaking. The rain held off long enough for me to get these shots.

The Hudson River waterfront in the thunderstorm.

A never to be repeated scene, and one of my best ever pictures.

In 2000 we made our first journey to India, and were accompanied by the Z135, the little Nikon and the Panasonic video camera. Below are some of the pictures I took:

Jill and I on the "Princess Diana" bench. Picture taken by a helpful self appointed guide, who attached himself to us.

An "iconic" view of the Taj Mahal, that nearly everyone takes.

The elephant ride in Jaipur, taking us from the fort back to the town, taken by a street photographer, who borrowed my camera, and luckily gave it back to me.

Jodhpur, the Blue City - taken from the fort which overlooks it

Udaipur, the Maharaja's Palace, which was also where we stayed

Prayer flags in the temple at Darjeeling

The view from the Windermere Hotel in Darjeeling

The view of the Himalayas which only appeared on the last day of the five we spent there

Sunset over the Ganges at Rajshahi, where we stayed with Julietta in Bangladesh

Jill and Julietta in Rajshahi with Jasmina her cook/housekeeper.

In November 1995 Canon introduced the EOS 50E with a great fanfare in the photographic press, which I used to read diligently while eating my sandwich at lunch time.

The EOS 50E, the last 35mm camera I bought for actually taking photographs

I am afraid I was overcome with desire to have it, a feeling that sometimes happens when you have access to more money than sense. I had convinced myself that it was really necessary for the firm to buy one, even though there was nothing wrong with the EOS 100 and 650 that were coping with the pictures we were taking for the catalogues. We produced additional leaflets probably every two years even after the main catalogue was finished. The business was still expanding and we were finding new items to sell all the time, and the only way to publicise them was with leaflets and handouts.

The new features of the camera were of course mainly cosmetic with its aluminium top plate, and the knobs and dials. The rest of the camera was still plastic but it did have a more retro feel. Also there was a move back to functions being controlled by dials and levers and away from having to scroll through menus. I bought it with the cheapest kit lens as in those days the tendency of buying the body only had not quite evolved; I took my prized 35-135 zoom lens off the EOS 100 and used it on the 50E. One interesting feature on the 50E was the eye-movement sensors built into the edge of the viewfinder surround, so that you could control the focus point by simply looking at it through the viewfinder. How clever is that? It also worked in the vertical position. Otherwise the camera had all the functions that were previously only available on much more expensive models and therefore made it irresistible.

The camera seldom came on holidays as we only had time for one holiday a year: that seemed to follow the pattern of going to America on business every other year, followed by a fortnight of relaxation then home on the QE2. The in-between years were spent in Europe by car, making calls on all our customers on the way. The journey usually started in Spain to see our Spanish customer in Barcelona, then around the coast eastwards to Italy to see our man in Viareggio near Pisa, and then back through Switzerland, Germany and Belgium with calls in each country. I still was taking video and it was much more convenient to take the Z135 Compact, on our first journey to India in 2000, and whose results were good enough for an album of 7"X5" prints and the occasional 18"X12" to frame and put on the wall.

For relaxation I did join the Penarth Camera Club for two years, but found that I did not really fit in. The club was very well established and had a clique of old timers who had been everywhere and done everything and a newcomer was treated as an unwanted interloper. Their main interest was in slide photography which did not appeal to me. Slides need a projector to view them and could not easily be made into prints. I liked to have a picture to hold in my hand, to show to people and to put in an album. At the club the only activity was endless slide shows of all the holidays to exotic locations that the members had been to. Then there were the slide 'battles' with other clubs in the area, involving visiting judges who were invited solely to make comments and find a winner. As nearly all my work was with colour prints I just had nothing to show and so could not take part. They never had any practical evenings or visits from speakers and in the end when the membership year had finished, I decided it was not for me and gave up. I went to evening classes in Dinas Powis and all these classes did was darkroom work, using black and white film, which I had not used for about 25 years. So that only lasted one year. But as the end of the millennium approached, digital was already looking to become affordable and a whole exciting new era was on the horizon.

Chapter 13: the digital era

Although we had been using computers at the factory since 1982 I had taken very little interest in them, except for the time when they went wrong, and in the early days that was pretty often. I would also wince at the bills that came in for fixing them - both the hardware and the software - but as long as they did their job I was content to leave it to others to actually operate them. If I needed any information, I had at least four girls there who would tell me what I wanted to know in a flash. So 'Why bother to learn?' was my attitude and 'Why keep a dog and bark yourself?' my maxim.

I was aware of the coming of digital cameras but they were outrageously expensive, produced pictures with a quality that could only be printed on 6"X 4" paper and needed a computer to work with the camera. So how could that possibly be of interest to me when I had cameras that were at the peak of 35mm development, and developing and printing had been perfected so that 36 7"X 5" prints could be had for about £4.00 or less and in an hour if needed.

So much for the negative aspect, but you cannot stand in the way of progress. As I have said before photography played a large part in our business with the production of catalogues and leaflets, and Angelina was very much involved with the marketing side, having taught herself to use the computer very competently. We became very involved with the printers (by the name of Qualitex in Cardiff) who we used and visited their offices regularly. We found that all the pictures they were using were being manipulated on their computers, having scanned the colour slides that I gave them. As I am always keen to save money, I thought it might be time to look into doing some of this work ourselves, using my skills as a photographer and Angelina's skills as a computer operator.

We had one range of parts in our programme that accounted for 25% of our sales which were devoted just to one maker of forklift trucks. In fact this was not dealt with in our main catalogue and had a separate brochure entirely. The one we were using in the late Nineties had been going for about 5 years and was becoming very out-of-date - so many extra new parts had become available that people were not ordering because they did not know that we had them. All this was long before information could be easily obtained as it can today from the internet. Engineers relied on having a file of grubby oil stained leaflets in their vans and brick-sized mobile phones to ring for parts to be ordered. So we set about planning a new leaflet and thought this was the time to invest in a digital camera; we could present the printer with pictures as computer files and so save them a lot of time and us expense in the production cost. The choice of a camera was not really very difficult. There was only one that looked in any way affordable and that was made by Olympus, a maker for whom I had a very high regard. Canon, Nikon and all the rest had cameras but these were three or more times the price, and much more than I wanted to spend on what was really an experiment that might not work.

At the time I was also not really aware of how fast digital cameras were going to evolve. We chose their Camedia C-800L, which had been on the market for a year or two and whose price was £1150. The camera was very simple to use and had practically no adjustments. It was intended as a point-and-shoot camera for amateurs although there must have been very few people prepared to pay that sort of money for such poor results. The sensor had a resolution of 0.81 Megapixels and the camera had a built in memory of I think 32 Megabytes, so that it could take about 36 pictures before they had to be downloaded to the computer. There were no memory cards at that time. It took 6 AA cells and you were lucky if these lasted as long as the memory. We used rechargeable batteries and after a few charges these lost their capacity fairly quickly too.

What drained the batteries the quickest was using the very small LCD screen at the back. This was only about 36 X 24mm in size and in bright light virtually unusable

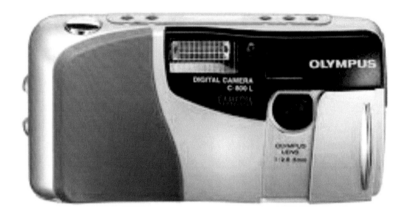

The Olympus Camedia C-800L, which has not yet been replaced in the collection. This is an internet picture.

We laid out the parts on the usual yellow cloth on the floor of the office and because I could not keep up with the consumption of batteries and the length of time to recharge them, decided that for lighting we would use two 500 watt security lights mounted on poles in order to flood the area with light. As the camera was on a tripod and had automatic exposure we hoped it would be able to cope. It did, but only after a fashion. The problem was that some pictures contained only small parts and could be taken from a distance of 3 or 4 feet; others had large parts that required the camera to be twice as far away. The camera had a fixed focal length lens and this was a problem that a zoom lens obviates. Although the background came up quite nice and yellow on the close up pictures, the further back we went the more it turned green and there was nothing we could do to change it.

Angelina had only a very basic program for manipulating the results on the computer as Photoshop cost about £700 and the Corel Draw that she had cost about £70. But you only get what you pay for and it certainly proved true in this case. So we did the best we could and handed the floppy disks to the printer. By this time the rather helpful fellow we dealt with at Qualitex (who had by now moved to Llanishen) was no longer there and the whole business had been sold to a company called Hackman somewhere in the Rhondda Valley with whom we had no real contact, other than with the original representative who called to see us. The results were pretty disappointing as they could not get rid of the green cast either and we were stuck with it.

This brochure came out in 2000 and it was only a short time later that we started to think about selling the business and there was no need for any more photography. When I eventually sold up the new owners said they wanted the camera as it was still in the books as an asset of £1150. Luckily they did not ask me for any of the other 35mm cameras that I had bought and I still have them in my collection. But the Camedia C-800L is only a memory.

Towards the end of 2002 the price of simple digital cameras had dropped to realistic levels and the number of Megapixels of resolution was rising too. I felt that I had to look into it. I went to see my old friend Steve from my Dixon days who was now working at Cameraland in the High Street Arcade and he did not have to work very hard to persuade me to hand over my credit card in exchange for an Olympus Camedia C-120.

A replacement for the Olympus Camedia C-120

I did not have this camera for very long and cannot remember very much about it. Essentially one slid open the front flap, composed the picture in the LCD screen at the back and pressed the button. Luckily it had a view finder which is essential in my opinion, as on a bright day whatever is on the screen is virtually invisible. It came on one holiday with us to Morocco in 2003. I have an album of this holiday and a file of the photographs that the C-120 took, and looking at both I note that the majority must have been taken on film with the Canon Z135. The latter was so much more versatile that I was not prepared to abandon film at this stage. Some of the digital pictures are reproduced below. The camera was handicapped by not having a zoom lens and the only control the user had was to override the automatic flash. It cost very nearly £200 too but this was a big decrease from its far inferior predecessor.

172

Above Jill, with the scarf we later bought. Below the "not very" old town in Agadir.

The house and gardens belonging to Yves St Laurent, which are open to the public

Spices on sale in the souk in Marrakesh

Although my camera collection was starting to grow at that time I did not think it would ever include digital cameras. So when Wayne told me in 2004 that they really needed a cheap camera to keep at the factory in case pictures need to be taken and sent to our partners in India, I seized the opportunity to sell him the C-120 and buy myself a newer and better one. When I asked in 2012 if he still had it I got a quizzical look and was told that it had long since departed for camera heaven up in the sky - or the skip which is probably more likely.

We had started the process of selling our company in the early autumn of 2002, after coming to the momentous decision during our holiday in Javea in Spain, and had reached agreement with the eventual purchaser in February 2003. We had the Moroccan holiday in April and then spent most of the ensuing months with our solicitor sorting out the details. Eventually a date for completion was set - August 4th - which also happened to be my birthday. This day came and went with the handover eventually taking place on August 5th. By the 6th I was retired and had quite a lot of cash stuffed in my pocket.....

So the thought did cross my mind that perhaps I could afford a 'proper' digital camera but the problem was what to buy. I spent several mornings of my now ample free time touring the 3 or 4 camera shops in Cardiff looking at what was available. I was prepared to spend between £500 and £1000 and so this ruled out the few single lens reflexes that were available from Canon and Nikon as they were three times my top limit. I was not really convinced with what I could find and not impressed at all with the electronic viewfinders that were available. But fate was kind to me and it was during these deliberations that I read in a magazine that Canon was about to launch a single lens reflex at an affordable price - the 300D. I went to see my friend Steve and to my surprise found he had just received his allocation of two that morning. It was not long before I was on

175

the way home clutching the box and my bank account was £850 lighter.

The Canon EOS 300D

It came with the standard kit lens, an 18-55mm zoom. This equates to 28-85mm in old money or 35mm terms. Everything else on it was the same as all my other Canons so very familiar. This camera now boasted 6.3 Megapixels which was well ahead of the game at the time, and I thought would serve me well for many years. This proved to be the case as it lasted for 5 years until newer and better Canons came along to tempt me.

The main holiday that this camera came on was the following year when we did the voyage through the Panama Canal on the QE2. We flew to New York and after a visit to my cousin Gusti (the last one as it turned out as she sadly died not long afterwards) boarded the ship at Pier 90. We sailed to Fort Lauderdale with the ship almost empty and thought *this is great!*. I had splashed out on a slightly better grade of cabin/restaurant too and we were set to enjoy the trip. In Fort Lauderdale about 2000 Americans got on and Jill wanted to get off there and then. I persuaded her that I did want to see the canal, and through gritted teeth she agreed to hang on. I think she cheered up once we got going to the more exotic locations like Curacao, Acapulco and Cabo San Lucas

The QE2, our favourite ship, just before departure from Wilhelmstedt in Curacao

On looking through the album of pictures of this holiday, I see that many more were taken on 35mm film with the Canon Z135. We have a videotape of the holiday and it was not feasible to carry the video camera, and more than one other cameras, and it appears that the Z135 was used more often, because it is so much smaller and lighter. The results from it are every bit as good. I am including a further selection taken with the 300D.

West-bound through the Gatun lock with a queue of ships following

Los Arcos at Cabo San Lucas

One of the pools at Hearst Castle mid-way between Los Angeles and San Francisco

Museum ships at San Francisco, with the same sailing ship from Penarth as in 1993

In the autumn of 2004, I went to India again for our mid-year board meeting with Exide and was asked to bring the camera to take some pictures of the factory which could be used on our stand at a forthcoming Materials Handling Exhibition at the NEC. They were enlarged to 3' X 2', framed and looked very good--especially when viewed from a distance!

Above and below, pictures of battery making machinery at Haldia.

The red oxide room, which is now no longer used, and a battery assembly line below.

181

After our return from America, and before the trip to India, I thought that it was time to leave 35mm behind and invest in a digital compact to complement the Canon 300D. At about this time we bought a new computer as the one I had before was a cast-off from the factory and pretty ancient and out of date. Computer development was moving just as fast as camera development and the requirements of the newer software demanded better and faster hardware. Along with the Canon 300D came a disc with Photoshop Elements on it and I was learning (slowly) how to manipulate and improve what the camera turned out - something that was not really possible with 35mm and using developing and printing labs to produce the prints. So it was a trawl of the shops again as I was still not well versed in internet shopping - if you wanted a camera you went to a shop and bought one. How times have changed.

I still had a soft spot for Olympus for compacts although I was not such a big fan of their bigger cameras. Also there is the question of lenses and once a maker has you in his clutches, it is hard to escape as there is no longer any interchangability between makers. In the end I came back to Cameraland and Steve had another wedge of cash from my pocket. I settled on an Olympus Camedia C-360 Zoom as it had all the features I wanted, was small enough not to be an encumbrance and had the all-important viewfinder as well as the LCD screen at the back. It boasted 3.2 megapixels, which was about par for the course in compacts at the time. It cost me £159 with a case and flash card thrown in as discount. Considering all the cameras I had bought from Steve over the years he was pretty unbending as far as prices went. He would not get away with it today anymore.

The Olympus Camedia C360, which Jill still uses today.

This camera has been in use continually ever since as I have passed it on to Jill and she is very happy with it. She says it is all she wants. Flick open the cover and press the button, the results are pretty well guaranteed to be acceptable. A bit of manipulation in Photoshop may be required though.

In 2005 the Megapixel race was really hotting up, and the Olympus at 3.2 was looking sickly. A camera that was heavily promoted at the time was made by Samsung (the V700) and this really caught my eye. I had just bought 2 Samsung flat screen TVs, had a Samsung mobile phone and was generally very impressed with their technical prowess.

The Samsung V 700

It was very nicely made from metal and had a solid feel to it. It also had a Schneider lens with a 3X zoom which gives the equivalent of 28mm X 85mm in 35mm terms. The screen at the back was still very small but it had a viewfinder and all the control I wanted for a point and shoot compact. I used this camera extensively for the next five years and it came on all our holidays over that period.

In 2005, we went on a tour of the Baltic capitals on the MV Discovery and some excellent pictures resulted, some due to the Olympus C-360 and some from the Canon 300D. I think some are worth printing and I have added my comments to each.

The Warship Vasa, built in 1626, which sank in Stockholm harbour 2000 meters into its maiden voyage. It was raised in the fifties and now has its own museum (taken with the Canon 300D)

The MV Van Gough leaving St Petersburg, picture taken after midnight! (taken with the 300D)

185

The Cathedral of the Spilt Blood in St Petersburg, where Emperor Alexander 11 was assassinated in 1881 (taken with the Canon 300D)

The Battleship Aurora, which played a decisive role in the Russian Revolution by firing one shot over the Winter Palace in 1917.The Tsar then surrendered. It is now berthed directly opposite to it (taken with the Canon 300D)

The fountains and gold statues at the Summer Palace near St Petersburg (taken with the Olympus C-360)

The MV Discovery moored at Tallinn Estonia on the way back (taken with the Olympus C-360)

We went to India in 2006 and the river/canal cruise from Amsterdam to Budapest. The following year we went to Corsica by car and then in August took our boat Q-dos to Ireland. In the autumn of 2007 it was back to India, and our memorable trip to the tigers in Ranthambhore National Park, then in 2008 our last motoring holiday in Sicily. The camera is still in use as I have lent it to Julietta, her camera having come to the end of its useful life. No doubt one day it will come back to me and be added to my collection.

In the summer of 2007, before Angelina and I went to India, I saw advertisements for a new Sigma lens with a big zoom range of 18mm-200mm, which is the equivalent of 28-335mm on a 35mm camera. More importantly though it had optical image stabilization. I had been finding that with increasing age, I can no longer hold the camera as steady as when I was younger, and getting sharp pictures at very long focal lengths was becoming impossible. So OS seemed to be the answer. I bought a lens from Camera Centre in Cardiff as soon as it became available. The trouble with being one of the first to buy anything is that you pay top price. Within a few weeks the price starts to drop and it is always best to wait a while....if you have the patience that is. But I wanted it for India so waiting was not an option.

*The 300D with the Sigma Zoom - shown normally
and at full stretch*

My investment was rewarded with some good shots of the elusive tigers, one of which came ambling towards us and crossed right in front of the jeep, then disappeared into the undergrowth. Luckily the camera worked well as there are no second chances in situations like that.

A very friendly tiger no more than 6 feet away.

Two new cameras came in 2009, and that brings the story right up to date. The first to arrive was a replacement for the Canon 300D. This was now 6 years old and in digital camera terms that is positively antediluvian. New cameras are launched roughly every year and when a replacement arrives, it instantly makes its predecessor look ancient. All the big makers do this and of course it keeps generating sales, as all keen photographers want the latest gear. So by keeping an eye on the advertisements in the camera magazines, I had noticed that the Canon 40D was falling in price and getting to the stage where it looked quite a bargain. Once the price starts to fall everyone knows that it is coming to the end of its production life - and a new model is just around the corner.

The Canon 40D

It was not necessary to buy a lens this time as I already had two. It was a big advance on the 300D. For a start it is made of magnesium alloy rather than plastic and has a very weighty feel to it. It has a really large 3"LCD screen on the back with 'live view', a feature that was just becoming available on single lens reflexes, and which I find extremely useful especially for taking pictures of my camera collection and Jill's paintings, which is the main use the camera gets. It had 'only' 10 megapixels, which of course is why the price was dropping, as the game had moved on and 15 was the new bench mark. Not surprisingly very soon after I had bought it, Canon announced the 50D which was virtually the same body, but with the larger pixel count. And at almost twice the price. I am quite happy with it though and think I did the right thing.

In the meantime Canon has announced the 60D but this has reverted to a plastic body. I had improved my buying strategy by this time too. I went on the internet and searched out the lowest price I could find for a legal camera - as opposed to a grey import which are quite plentiful. The best price as I recall was £499 which included a cash-back offer from Canon of £100. I went into town and the first shop I went into was Jessop's, being nearest to where I parked the scooter. They had a demonstration model to handle and I was totally convinced that it was what I wanted. The marked price was about £100 more than my target, so I told the chap that I would have it for £499. To my surprise, after consulting his computer he agreed to sell me a body only. Then there did not seem much point in going to see any other shops - possibly I could have squeezed a few more pounds off but one can be too greedy and once you have said the price you wanted to pay, it is hard to drop it down any more. I was quite happy with my purchase. As expected a few weeks later the 50D came on the market at around £800 and the price of the 40D dropped again. But how long can one wait and what is the point?

And so we come to the final new camera purchase in my story. I am fairly sure it will not be the last but brings me up to date. I was still using the Samsung as a compact and general workhorse but it was falling behind in the technology developments that were available. I had noticed that Canon had a very highly specified compact called the Powershot G9 and I went to look at one. At the same time I bought some magazines to read the reports and study prices. Just as well that I did as the editorial revealed that Canon was going to launch the G10 the following week. This indeed happened and the G10, whilst looking superficially similar, had many worthwhile improvements. I could not go to look at one but instead bought one on the internet. At the time the shop price was around £450 but Warehouse Express was offering it for £341 and so I bought it, hoping they were a reputable company. When it arrived there was no instruction book, only a CD with it on. This made me suspicious that it may have been a grey import but no matter, the camera works very well and as it is basically very similar to the 40D (for which I have a book) I have managed to work out how to use it without any problems.

The Canon G10

The camera has the all-important viewfinder as well as a 3" screen at the back. It also has 14.7 megapixels which was at the top of the league table at the time. What also pleased me was that most of the settings were done with knobs rather than scrolling through menus which always necessitate me finding my reading glasses, by which time the photo-opportunity has often passed. Of course six months later Canon announced the G11 but to my mind this was a step back, as they had reduced the pixel count to 10. The G12 followed very soon after and this had a fold out screen to warrant the name change. Finally just recently, they announced the G1X, which has 14.7 megapixels again, but loses some of the knob controls. I think I will stick with the G10 until something much better comes along.

In 2011 I managed to persuade Jill that we would really enjoy another cruise, this time going northwards, round the North Cape and ending in Archangel. Unfortunately it was on the MV Discovery again and, just as lightning does not strike the same spot twice, this cruise was nowhere near as enjoyable as the one to the Baltic. The main problem was with the other passengers who we found irksome and irritating. Perhaps we are getting older and more grumpy, but we came to the conclusion that cruising was no longer for us. It has been suggested that it may be better on a ship that is not so obviously past its prime and getting very shabby. I do not think I will ever manage to convince Jill about this again and for that matter myself too. I did take both the 40D and the G10 and some quite nice pictures resulted. A few samples follow.

Jill at the northernmost point on mainland Europe with the sculpture to signify this. Taken at 10.00pm (with the Canon 40D) and it was quite cold too.

The monastery on the Solovetsky Islands, which Stalin used as his first Gulag. 16,000 prisoners were murdered or died from starvation and disease (taken with the Canon G10)

Picture taken (with the Canon 40D) after midnight whilst heading south through the fiords.

Jill in the lounge after midnight, which accounts for the absence of other passengers - a rare occurrence (taken with the Canon 40D)

The MV Discovery moored at Alvesund on the last stop of the return leg (taken with the Canon 40D)

Chapter 14: the camera collection

The camera collection evolved because of my reluctance to throw anything away. This probably explains why I have an attic full of old radios, stereos, tape recorders etc, which will probably never be used again, but I just do not have the heart to chuck them all into a skip. Fortunately I have no wish to start a collection of such items. But equally fortunately after about 1978 when I sold the Zenith C after buying the Carena in Swansea, I have kept every camera. The two that were still lurking in the back of the cupboard were the Retina I bought in Birmingham in the early sixties, and the Kiev which was almost brand new. Then in 1992, for no reason that I can recollect, I was leafing through the back of Amateur Photographer magazine, and came across an advertisement from Ffordes of Southend-on-Sea who took a double page spread every week and offered a range of early Leicas, at what seemed like very reasonable prices. I rang them and a very friendly chap said that if I gave him a credit card number he would send a Leica 111A with f.3.5 Elmar lens on seven days approval. It came next day and of course there was no chance that I would send it back once I had it in my hands. I am sure he knew that. I paid £195 and I think it is worth nearly double that today 20 years on. I put a film through it and it produced very acceptable results.

But I am afraid that at that time I had a view which has not changed today - that to take photographs you need the most sophisticated camera available which makes taking the picture as easy and automatic as possible. This is so that you can concentrate on the picture rather than the mechanics of operating the camera. There is always something that you have forgotten to do before you press the button and it becomes very frustrating. Take the case of the Leica. To load the film is an art in itself. The film leader has to be re-trimmed with a pair of scissors to a special template. It is impossible to describe how difficult it is to slide the film, cassette and take-up spool, all into a narrow slot at the back of the camera, from the base upwards. This requires two hands with the camera balanced on your lap. Luckily the Zenith had the same system as it was a copy of the Leica. You then had to remember to wind the film, use a separate exposure meter to determine the exposure, set the aperture and shutter speed, focus with the rangefinder, press the button and after 36 exposures rewind the film.

At the time when I bought the Leica 111A, I already had the Canon EOS650 with its automatic loading, auto focus, auto-exposure and auto rewind when the film is finished. My feelings, not shared by everyone I must add, is that I like collecting cameras as items of engineering excellence and design, relevant to the time when they were made, rather than picture-taking tools. The pictures that they took in the past I value greatly for their historical interest, but for taking pictures today, give me the latest digital masterpiece every time.

The next landmark event was when I spotted a Retinette 11A in the Tenovus Charity shop in Penarth with a price of £16, which seemed very reasonable. I bought it and put it in the cupboard with all the other cameras I had acquired, and had made into a display. On a business trip to London I had a day with an early morning meeting, (breakfast with Mr Ganguly, the CEO of Exide Industries Ltd) which was over much sooner than I had expected, and I had a train home booked mid-afternoon. So having not very much to do, I went to Pied Bull Yard near the British Museum, where there was a collection of second-hand camera shops, led by Jessop's Classics. My enthusiasm was immediately fired and I bought five for my collection. Sadly only two still remain as I went off totally in the wrong direction to what I have eventually focused on. But the ones I did not want have all sold not for quite what I gave for them - in my ignorance I paid full retail price and you can never hope to make money on something bought from a retailer.

In 2001 I saw an advertisement in the Amateur Photographer magazine for Photographica for the first time and decided to go. To quote the well used phrase, *I thought I had died and woken up in heaven.* Here was Pied Bull Yard a hundredfold bigger and with cameras at unbelievable prices. Even better everyone was haggling and no-one paid the price on the ticket. The first camera I bought was the Zeiss Super Nettle because it was the camera my father had when I was very young, which I was never allowed to touch and had always lusted after. I also bought an Olympus OM-1 because I had always admired it and could never afford one. Also an Olympus Trip 35 because it was so cheap at £10. I also joined the Photographic Collectors Club who were the organisers of the event. I think I have only missed one Photographica in the ensuing years.

As time went on I gradually decided on what I was going to collect. The initial focus was on the cameras that I had once had and through financial circumstances had sold, but also the cameras that my father once had. The story of his last camera, the Retina Reflex, has already been told: its journey to Vienna and back and now has pride of place in the collection. So my focus became primarily on Retinas and Zeiss 35mm, dating between 1932, and 1970, by which time the German camera industry had been forced to cease production due to pressure from the Far East. Once I had the items on my shelves the collecting bug was still biting me, and as I had bought a few Olympus cameras along the way expanded the collection to include their more valuable and collectible cameras, especially the ones they brought out to overwhelm the Germans.

At the time I was an enthusiastic user of their compact cameras too. I also had a fair number of Canons and so bought some historically interesting models that they had made in the post-war years. I never developed the Leica strain of the collecting bug as the financial cost is too great, even for someone suffering from the bite of the bug like me. But on a trip to the north of Scotland, I called at Fforde's new shop in Beauly near Inverness and fell for a Leica M3, which I had always admired. A couple of Leica lenses followed from various fairs. I collected the Carl Zeiss Werras, because they are of a unique design and made by the original Zeiss Company, and I think may have potential as an investment. Lastly the Akarettes, because that was my first real camera and I had a soft spot for them.

In the "odds and ends" section I have a few cameras that have caught my imagination over the years, and one or two are worth mentioning. Both as it happens are Kodak, as I have a particular affection for this company. The Kodak Bantam Special was a futuristic design that first appeared on the scene in 1936, and was made until 1948. It was widely acknowledged to be a masterpiece of Art-Deco design. It used 828 film, which was really 35mm film without the perforation, and with a paper backing. It was a folding camera, with a black enamelled body with white lines, and had a chunky f.2.0/50 Ektar lens, in a Compur Rapid shutter. It also had a coupled rangefinder. It held a special place in my imagination because I remember from the time during the war finding in the bookcase a Kodak Catalogue from pre-war days which had this camera on the front cover, and it was my dream to have one. That dream came true in 2005, when I bought one at Photographica, for £200. That was the asking price, and unusually the vendor would not budge an inch. Such is the demand for collectible cameras.

The Kodak Bantam Special

Another interesting camera that I bought more recently is the Kodak Advantix Preview. I thought this was interesting as it illustrated another cul-de-sac which Kodak went up in their determination to persist with film cameras in the face of the onslaught of digital imaging. They thought they would combine the best of both, and so keep selling film, which has always been their main focus, but still pander to the digital revolution. You cannot stop progress though, and digital was improving by leaps and bounds, and film was going nowhere anymore. So the whole thing proved to be pointless exercise, and very few were made.

The unique feature was that although the camera took pictures on APS film, it had an LCD screen on the back which briefly showed what you had just taken. This allowed you to instantly judge if the picture was acceptable or whether it needed to be deleted and taken again. It also enabled the user to decide the number of copies to be printed when the film was developed. The camera came out in 2001, and sold in America for $350. Of course with the benefit of hindsight we can see this was when digital was still in its infancy, and who could have predicted the speed at which it was to develop both with regard to the megapixel count, and the increase in memory capacity. This camera came out at the time when I paid £1150 for the

Olympus Camedia C-800L, and the limitations of that camera have already been dealt with in the previous chapter. Someone showed me one at a club meeting in Taunton, and although he was a dealer, would not sell it to me. Of course that made me want to buy one, and a bit of persistence on e-bay yielded success, and I bought one still in its original box and hardly used for £20. I am hoping that in 50 years time it may be regarded as a classic like the Bantam Special. On the other hand it may just been seen as a folly that led nowhere.

The Kodak Advantix Preview.

The Photographic Collectors Club organized coach trips to the French Fair at Bievres for 3 years running, so I went there and came back well laden each time. It also gave us a weekend in Paris, which is always enjoyable. Jill and I have also been to the Dutch Fair at Houten and came back with a good haul.

However the cost of getting there is rather daunting and only includes two nights on the car ferry and a lot of driving. I am doubtful that it is cost-effective.

In April 2007 I saw an appeal in Tailboard, the Club's newsletter for a volunteer to take on the role of secretary, and I thought that as I had been in a similar role twice before in my life (with the SWAC car club and more recently the Marina berth-holders) I would offer my services, since I had both the time and the interest. I had a meeting with Roger Bradley the then Chairman, and David Balfour the Treasurer at Photographica in the May, and they were happy to have me aboard. I have been doing the job ever since and also played a much more active role in the meetings of the South West region in Taunton. It is a long way to go but I enjoy it.

Finally we come to e-bay. I have to admit that I am an addict, along with millions of others. But it has been the biggest source of cameras for me especially for the cheaper bulk of the collection. All my really good items though came from the fairs or sales tables at club meetings. My really expensive Zeiss items came from a dealer, Peter Loy (who always takes a table at Photographica and the club's Annual General Meeting). It is risky buying expensive items from unknown sources. The next few pages show the whole collection as it is in Spring 2012.

The Retina collection.

1. Retina 1 -117

2. Retina 1 -118

3. Retina 1-119

4. Retina 1-119

5. Retina 1-141

6. Retina 1-143

7. Retina 1-148

8. Retina 1-149

9. Retina 1-O1O

10.Retina 1-010

11.Retina 1a-015

12.Retina 1b-018

13.Retina 1B-019-0

14.Retina 1B-019

15.Retina 11-142

16.Retina 11a-150

17.Retina 11a-016

18.Retina 11c-020

19.Retina 11C-029

20.Retina 111c-021

21.Retina 111C-028

22.Retina Reflex-025

23.Retina Reflex S-034

24. Tele Xenar Lens

25.Retina Reflex 3-041

26.Retina Reflex 4-051

27.Retina 1BS-040

28.Retina 11S-024

29.Retina 111S-027

30.Retina Lenses

31.Retina A-matic 1-038

32. Retina A-matic 11-032

33.Retina A-matic 111-039

34.Retina 1F-046

35.Retina 11F-047

36.Retina S1-060

37.Retina S2-061

The Retinette collection.

38.Retinette-147

39.Retinette-160

40.Retinette-012- Ennatar

41.Retinette-012-Reomar

42.Retinette-017

43.Retinette-022

44.Retinette 1-030

45.Retinette 1A-042

46.Retinette 1B-037

47.Retinette 1B-045

48.Retinette 11-026

49.Retinette 11A-036

50.Retinette 11B-031

The Akarette collection

1.Akarette 0

2.Akarette 11

3.Akarelle

4.Akarette 11

5.Westron Lens

6.Akarex 1

7.Akarex 111

8.Arette P

9.Arette 1A

10.Arette 1B

11.Arette DN

12.Arette P

13.Arette C

14.Arette Auto SE

| 1.Tenax 1 | 2.Tenax 11 | 3.Super Nettel | 4.Nettax | 5.Contax 1F |

| 6.Contax 11 | 7.Contax 111 | 8.Contax 11A | 9.Contax 111A | 10.Sonnar Lens |

| 11.Continette | 12.Contina J | 13.Contina L | 14.Contina LK | 15.Contina 1A |

| 16.Contina 1C | 17.Contina 11A | 18.Contina 111 | 19.Contina-matic | 20.Contina 1 Folding |

| 21.Contina 11 Folding | 22.Contessa 35 | 23.Contaflex 1 | 24.Contaflex 11 | 25.Contaflex 111 |

| 26.Contaflex 1V | 27.Contaflex Super | 28.Contaflex Super BC | 29.Contaflex S | 30.Pro-Tessar Lenses |

| 31.Contaflex 126 | 32.Contarex Bullseye | 33.Sonnar Lens | 34.Icarex 35CS | 35.Icarex 35S BM |

Zeiss continued

36.Contessa LK

37.Contessa LKE

38.Contessa SE

39.Contessa SBE

40.Contessa-matic E

41.Contessa-matic

42.Contessa-mat STE

43.Tenax Automatic

44.Symbolica

45.Colora

46.Colora Late

47.Contessa S-310

48.Contessa S-312

49.Contax F

50.Baby Box Tengor

51.Ikonta B

The Werra collection

1.Werra 1B

2.Werra 1E

3.Werra 11

4.Werra 111

5.Werra 1V

6.Werra 3E

7.Werra V

8.Werramat E

9.Werramatic E & lenses

The Canon collection

1.Canon A1
2.Canon AE-1
3.EOS 650
4.EOS 100
5.EOS 50E

6.EOS 300
7.Sureshot Z135
8.Sureshot A1
9.Sureshot Telemax
10.Sureshot Supreme

11.Sureshot EX
12.Canon 1VSB
13.Canon P
14.Canon 7
15.Canon V1-L

16.Canonet QL17
17.Canonet QL25
18.Canonet Basic
19.Canonet G111-QL19
20.Canonet 28

21.Canon A35F
22.Canon AF35M
23.Canon 300D
24.Canon 40D
25.Canon G10

26.Tamron FD Lenses

The Leica collection

1.Leica 111A
2.Elmar 90mm
3.Leica M3
4.Hector 135mm
5. Leicameter

209

The Olympus collection

1.Olympus OM-1MD

2.Olympus OM-2N

3.Olympus OM-3

4.Olympus OM-4

5.Olympus OM-10

6.Olympus OM-20

7.Olympus OM-30

8.Olympus OM-40

9.Olympus OM 707

10.Olympus OM101

11.Olympus OM-1TR

12.Olympus Lenses

13.Olympus Ace

14.Olympus Trip 35

15.Olympus 35EC

16.Olympus 35ECR

17.Olympus 35SP

18.Olympus 35RC

19.Olympus 35RD

20.Olympus 35ED

21.Olympus 35DC

22.Olympus Autoeye 11

Olympus continued

23.Olympus Trip AF Mini

24.Olympus Trip MD

25.Olympus Trip XB400

26.Olympus XA

27.Olympus XA 1

28.Olympus XA 2

29.Olympus XA 2 Red

30.Olympus XA 3

31.Olympus XA 4

32.Olympus Mju-1

33.Olympus Mju-11

34.Olympus Mju-111-150

35.Olympus Superzoom 76G

36.Olympus Superzoom 110

37.Olympus Superzoom 210

38.Olympus AM-100

39.Olympus AF-1 Mini QD

40.Olympus AF 1

41.Olympus AF-10 Super

42. Olympus Camedia C-360

The Odds and Ends

9. Carena SRH 101

10.Kodak Bantam SP

11.Kodak Advantix Preview

12. Kodak Beau Brownie

13.No 3A Autographic

14.Kodak Pocket 1A

15.Kodak Folder

16 Half Plate Field Camera

17.Rondo 8mm Cine

18. Panasonic Video

19.Weston Euro-master

20. Exposure meter etc.

21. Samsung V700

211

Epilogue

Writing this book has been a very pleasant stroll down memory lane and reminded me of events that had been almost forgotten, with all that has happened in the years between. I have written it mainly for the benefit of our family in the hope that it may be passed on to future generations. Simply because a book is more likely to survive than a plastic bag full of old photographs that Jill had the foresight to keep, and which have been so useful for all three books. I am sure that all the albums of holiday photographs (and there are about sixty in all) will probably be consigned to a skip after my demise, but hopefully a small volume like this will be more enduring.

The chapter on the camera collection is maybe just a vanity exercise, but for the last five years at least it has been my hobby and given me much pleasure. As happens on *The Antiques Roadshow* if I were asked the question what camera I would save if our house was ever on fire it would have to be my father's Retina Reflex.